Understanding Depression

Series Editor: Cara Acred

Volume 265

Independence Educational Publishers

First published by Independence Educational Publishers

The Studio, High Green

Great Shelford

Cambridge CB22 5EG

England

© Independence 2014

British Library Cataloguing in Publication Data

Understanding depression. -- (Issues ; 265)
1. Depression, Mental. 2. Depression, Mental--Treatment.
I. Series II. Acred, Cara editor.
616.8'527-dc23

ISBN-13: 9781861686800

Printed in Great Britain
MWL Print Group Ltd

Contents

Chapter 1: What is depression?

Depression	1
Is depression a disability?	5
Stigma and discrimination	6
Depression is NOT a mental illness	8
Glenn Close: 'I feel shame I didn't pay attention to my bipolar sister'	9
Five ways to tackle SAD	11
Postnatal depression	12
Computer light at night 'causes depression', study suggests	13
Scientists find revolutionary 'biomarker' for clinical depression in teenage boys	14
Mental health warning for jobless young	15
Half of teens outgrow depression and anxiety	16
Negative effects of social networking	18

Chapter 2: Coping and treatment

Antidepressants	19
Pros and cons of medication	21
Depression over-diagnosed and over-treated	23
Depression: alternatives to drug treatment	24
Talking therapy	26
Depression and cognitive behavioural therapy	27
Males think that talking about problems is a waste of time	28
Depression symptoms may be improved by acupuncture or counselling	29
Surfing on prescription helps kids at breaking point	30
Self-help books aid depression	31
UK study into whether physical activity aids depression finds no additional benefit	32
Why the object of exercise is not just a physical one: regular exercise lowers depression risk by up to 30 per cent	33
Exercise for depression	33
'I run to boost my mood'	34
Green cities provide a mental health boost that lasts	35
What is SPARX?	36
Great dream	38

Key facts	40
Glossary	41
Assignments	42
Index	43
Acknowledgements	44

Introduction

Understanding Depression is Volume 265 in the ***ISSUES*** series. The aim of the series is to offer current, diverse information about important issues in our world, from a UK perspective.

ABOUT UNDERSTANDING DEPRESSION

47% of people know someone who has suffered from depression, yet many of us struggle to understand its causes and symptoms. This book looks at the definitions of depression, its varying forms and its causes. *Understanding Depression* also considers coping techniques and treatments, featuring a range of articles that will educate the reader and stimulate debate around this seldom talked about topic.

OUR SOURCES

Titles in the ***ISSUES*** series are designed to function as educational resource books, providing a balanced overview of a specific subject.

The information in our books is comprised of facts, articles and opinions from many different sources, including:

⇨ Newspaper reports and opinion pieces

⇨ Website factsheets

⇨ Magazine and journal articles

⇨ Statistics and surveys

⇨ Government reports

⇨ Literature from special interest groups

A NOTE ON CRITICAL EVALUATION

Because the information reprinted here is from a number of different sources, readers should bear in mind the origin of the text and whether the source is likely to have a particular bias when presenting information (or when conducting their research). It is hoped that, as you read about the many aspects of the issues explored in this book, you will critically evaluate the information presented.

It is important that you decide whether you are being presented with facts or opinions. Does the writer give a biased or unbiased report? If an opinion is being expressed, do you agree with the writer? Is there potential bias to the 'facts' or statistics behind an article?

ASSIGNMENTS

In the back of this book, you will find a selection of assignments designed to help you engage with the articles you have been reading and to explore your own opinions. Some tasks will take longer than others and there is a mixture of design, writing and research-based activities that you can complete alone or in a group.

FURTHER RESEARCH

At the end of each article we have listed its source and a website that you can visit if you would like to conduct your own research. Please remember to critically evaluate any sources that you consult and consider whether the information you are viewing is accurate and unbiased.

Useful weblinks

www.actionforhappiness.org

www.actionondepression.org

www.depressionalliance.org

www.depressionuk.org

www.journeysonline.org.uk

www.mentalhealth.org.uk

www.mentalhealthy.co.uk

www.mind.org.uk

www.nhs.uk – (search for 'depression' or 'Moodzone')

www.reachout.com

www.sparx.org.nz

www.studentsagainstdepression.org

www.thecalmzone.net

Depression

mental
health
foundation

Depression is a common mental disorder that causes people to experience depressed mood, loss of interest or pleasure, feelings of guilt or low self-worth, disturbed sleep or appetite, low energy and poor concentration.

Depression is different from feeling down or sad. Unhappiness is something which everyone feels at one time or another, usually due to a particular cause. A person suffering from depression will experience intense emotions of anxiety, hopelessness, negativity and helplessness, and the feelings stay with them instead of going away.

Depression can happen to anyone. Many successful and famous people who seem to have everything going for them battle with this problem. Depression also affects people of every age.

Half of the people who have depression will only experience it once but for the other half it will happen again. The length of time that it takes to recover ranges from around six months to a year or more.

Living with depression is difficult for those who suffer from it and for their family, friends and colleagues. It can be difficult to know if you are depressed and what you can do about it.

Signs and symptoms of depression

⇨ Tiredness and loss of energy.

⇨ Sadness that doesn't go away.

⇨ Loss of self-confidence and self-esteem.

⇨ Difficulty concentrating.

⇨ Not being able to enjoy things that are usually pleasurable or interesting.

⇨ Feeling anxious all the time.

⇨ Avoiding other people, sometimes even your close friends.

⇨ Feelings of helplessness and hopelessness.

⇨ Sleeping problems – difficulties in getting off to sleep or waking up much earlier than usual.

⇨ Very strong feelings of guilt or worthlessness.

⇨ Finding it hard to function at work/college/school.

⇨ Loss of appetite.

⇨ Loss of sex drive and/or sexual problems.

⇨ Physical aches and pains.

⇨ Thinking about suicide and death.

⇨ Self-harm.

If you experience four or more of these symptoms for most of the day – every day – for more than two weeks, you should seek help from your GP.

What causes depression?

Depression can happen suddenly as a result of physical illness, experiences dating back to childhood, unemployment, bereavement, family problems or other life-changing events.

Examples of chronic illnesses linked to depression include heart disease, back pain and cancer. Pituitary damage, a treatable condition which frequently follows head injuries, may also lead to depression.

Sometimes, there may be no clear reason for your depression but, whatever the original cause, identifying what may affect how you feel and the things that are likely to trigger depression is an important first step.

Types of depression

There are several types of depression, some of which are listed below.

Mild depression

Depression is described as mild when it has a limited negative effect on your daily life. For example, you may have difficulty concentrating at work or motivating yourself to do the things you normally enjoy.

Major depression

Major depression interferes with an individual's daily life – with eating, sleeping and other everyday activities. Some people may experience only one episode but it is more common to experience several episodes in a lifetime. It can lead to hospital admission, if the person is so unwell they are at risk of harm to themselves.

Bipolar disorder

The mood swings in bipolar disorder can be extreme – from highs, where the individual feels extremely elated and indestructible, to lows, where they may experience complete despair, lethargy and suicidal feelings. Sometimes people have very severe symptoms where they cannot make sense of their world and do things that seem odd or illogical.

Postnatal depression

Many new mothers experience what are sometimes called 'baby blues' a few days after the birth. These feelings of anxiety and lack of confidence are very distressing but in most cases last only a couple of weeks. Postnatal depression is more intense and lasts longer. It can leave new mothers feeling completely overwhelmed, inadequate and unable to cope. They may have problems sleeping, panic attacks or an intense fear of dying.

They may also experience negative feelings towards their child. It affects one in ten mothers and usually begins two to three weeks after the birth.

Seasonal Affective Disorder (SAD)

SAD is associated with the start of winter and can last until spring when longer days bring more daylight. When it is mild, it is sometimes called 'winter blues'. SAD can make the sufferer feel anxious, stressed and depressed. It may interfere with their moods and with their sleeping and eating patterns.

Taking control of your depression

Depression often makes you feel helpless. Taking action to make yourself feel more in control will have a positive effect, whether it's going to see your GP for treatment, joining a gym, going for daily walks, or doing something that you are interested in or good at. If you don't feel up to starting something new or joining a local group on your own, ask a friend to come with you.

There are many things you can do to help manage your symptoms and a wide range of treatments, both medical and non-medical, available through your GP.

The upcoming sections should help you to work out what you could be doing yourself and what information or support you may want to ask your GP about.

How you see yourself

The way you think about yourself will affect your frame of mind and feelings of depression. It is common to have feelings of worthlessness or guilt with depression. Try to be aware of any negative thoughts you have about yourself and how they might be affecting how you see yourself and how you feel. If you can, try to think

about how realistic these thoughts are and how you might change them into something more positive. You can speak to your GP about getting counselling or cognitive therapy.

Social networks

If you feel depressed it can be difficult to be sociable. Loneliness may make you feel worse, so it's important to keep in touch with friends and family. Having people around you or groups that you are involved in will help to reduce feelings of isolation.

If you do not have many social networks you could find out about local community groups or befriending schemes from your local library or ask at your GP surgery.

Worries about work, money or a legal situation

Making sure that you do not feel overwhelmed by your work responsibilities is important because it gives you a sense of being in control. It's important to make time for yourself to do things you want to do or to be with friends and family.

⇨ If you're struggling to cope with work pressures and you have access to an occupational health department, you can speak to them about how you are feeling. They may be able to help you to review your work commitments or address specific issues that are affecting your work.

⇨ If you are having financial difficulties, speak to your local Citizens Advice Bureau about how you might get financial help.

⇨ National Debtline provides free, confidential and independent advice for people with debt problems. If you are out of work or want to change your job, your local job centre may offer support in finding work.

Both the Citizens Advice Bureau and your local social services department can also help you with advice about benefits if you are unemployed or unable to work because of depression.

Where possible, you should always try to keep working. This is because people with depression often find that having something meaningful to do and a reason to get up in the

"It's a sensation of being afraid all the time but not even knowing what it is that you're afraid of."

Andrew Solomon

morning is very helpful. Being with work colleagues, having a routine to the day, and the sense of achievement in getting a job done are all good for your mental health.

Close relationships

Problems with close personal relationships can have a devastating effect on how you feel about yourself and the world. If you are struggling to cope with a difficult relationship or your depression is causing problems in your relationship you can contact Relate on 0845 456 1310. Relate helps all couples, whether or not they are married, including couples in same-sex relationships. Or you could speak to your GP or practice nurse about getting other forms of relationship counselling.

Physical activity

There is good evidence that exercise can lift your mood because it can take your mind off your depression as well as stimulate the release of endorphins in the brain. Endorphins are neurotransmitters produced in the pituitary gland in the brain that produce feelings of happiness.

If you have mild or moderate depression your GP might recommend you to join an exercise referral scheme. Ideally you should be aiming to take 50 minutes of exercise three to five times a week. You can break this time down into shorter periods to fit it into your everyday life.

If you want advice about what exercise you should be doing and how it might help your depression, speak to your GP or practice nurse.

Diet

Some studies have suggested a link between what you eat and depression, but there isn't enough conclusive evidence to say whether or not it can definitely make a difference. There is some evidence that foods that are rich in some essential fatty acids found in oily fish, like mackerel, salmon, herring, sardines, kippers and fresh tuna can help to relieve depression.

Whether there is a direct link or not, eating healthily will help you generally feel better and give you more energy, especially if you are also exercising.

Avoiding alcohol and drugs

Alcohol acts as a depressant on the brain. If you drink too much or too often, you are more likely to become depressed. If you are already suffering from depression, drinking alcohol can make you feel worse instead of better. With such a vicious circle it is best to drink moderately, if at all. Recreational drugs should also be avoided.

Managing anxiety

Around half of those people who experience depression will also experience anxiety. Taking steps to manage your anxiety can help give you the mental space to begin to deal with your depression. Talking about what is making you anxious, as well as a healthy diet and exercising, will all help you to control your anxiety.

Some people, especially those with mild depression, find that relaxation techniques such as massage and yoga help them to manage their anxiety.

Complementary medicine

There is some evidence that St John's Wort can help with mild to moderate depression. However, this drug is known to interact with other substances so you need to get advice from a pharmacist or other health professional before taking it.

Getting help

The first step in getting treatment will normally be to visit your GP practice. They will ask you a number of questions about how your depression is affecting you mentally and physically.

The first appointment can feel difficult so it might be helpful if you write down what you have been experiencing before you go. Make a note of any questions or worries you might have. Some people find it helpful to take a friend or family member.

It is important that you and your doctor agree how best to treat your problems.

Being as open as you can about your symptoms and how they are affecting you will really help. Your GP may suggest you see a specialist such as a mental health nurse, psychiatrist or psychologist.

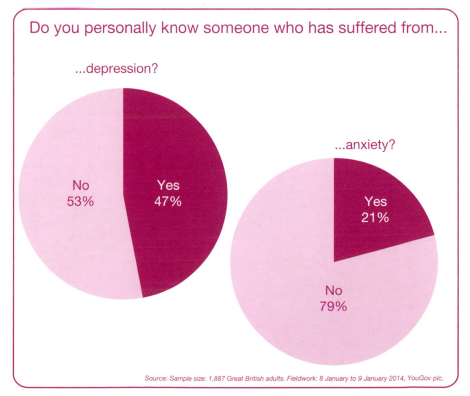

Do you personally know someone who has suffered from...

...depression?

No 53% Yes 47%

...anxiety?

Yes 21%

No 79%

Source: Sample size: 1,887 Great British adults. Fieldwork: 8 January to 9 January 2014, YouGov plc.

For mild depression, medication is not recommended because the risks could outweigh the benefits. Your GP has guidelines for treating depression and these recommend 'watchful waiting' initially, to see if the depression goes away. Using some of the self-help techniques listed above can help and your GP surgery can offer you support.

Talking therapies

Talking therapies such as cognitive behavioural therapy (CBT) and some forms of counselling and psychotherapy work well for depression, although you may have to wait to see a therapist on the NHS. You can pay to see someone privately and your GP may be able to recommend someone. Always check that any private therapist is registered with a professional body.

There are several different kinds of talking therapy. Your GP can advise you about which you might find most helpful.

⇨ Counselling gives people the chance to talk through everyday issues that may be causing depression and to develop strategies for resolving them.

⇨ Cognitive therapy (sometimes called cognitive behavioural therapy or CBT) addresses the way you think and how this can cause depression. It teaches you skills to identify patterns of behaviour and thinking that are causing you problems and change them.

⇨ Psychotherapy can be more intensive than counselling although people and organisations often use these terms interchangeably. It often looks at how past experience may be affecting your life now, so it may involve delving deeply into early experiences and key relationships. This may take more time, although shorter more focused ways of doing this have also been developed. Interpersonal therapy focuses on how you relate and behave towards others. It helps you to build a better self-image and communicate more effectively with others.

In many cases your GP will recommend antidepressants, either on their own or in combination with talking therapies. Antidepressants do work for many people but inevitably they do have side effects. You can discuss these with your GP.

About medication

Medication will not always be the first choice, especially if your depression is mild. There are a number of different types of antidepressants available. Your GP can explain which they believe is the best for you and why. What your doctor prescribes will depend on the type and severity of depression you have. If you experience problems from your medicine or have any concerns, speak to your GP.

If one medication does not work you may be prescribed something else. However, it takes a few weeks before your medicine starts to work so you need to allow enough time to see if it is going to be effective.

It is important that you take the medicine for the length of time recommended by your GP. If you come off your medicine too soon (even if you feel better) this can lead to a relapse where the depression returns. As a rough guide, you will usually have to remain on treatment for at least six to nine months and in many cases it could be longer. You need to follow your GP's advice when you are coming off your medicine as it can be harmful if this is done too quickly.

⇨ The above information is reprinted with kind permission from the Mental Health Foundation. Please visit www.mentalhealth.org.uk for further information.

© Mental Health Foundation 2014

Is depression a disability?

Depression can (but does not always) have legal status as a disability. Much depends on the severity of the depression, the length of the episode, and any past history of depression.

The Disability Discrimination Act (DDA) 1995 and 2005 give disabled people the right not to be discriminated against in:

⇨ Employment

⇨ Education

⇨ Access to goods, facilities and services, including larger private clubs and land-based transport services

⇨ Buying or renting land or property, including making it easier for disabled people to rent property and for tenants to make disability-related adaptations

⇨ Functions of public bodies, for example issuing of licences.

When is depression a disability?

The DDA defines a 'disabled person' as: a person with 'a physical or mental impairment which has a substantial and long-term adverse effect on his/her ability to carry out normal day-to-day activities'. In order to qualify as being disabled, someone with depression must show that:

⇨ S/he has a recognised 'mental impairment'

⇨ It is a long-term condition

⇨ It is severe enough to have an impact on his/her ability to function day-to-day.

All three conditions must be met for a person to be considered disabled.

Depression qualifies as a 'mental impairment' within the terms of DDA because it is a condition recognised by a respected body of medical opinion. 'Stress', for example, would not qualify a 'mental impairment', since it is not recognised as a medical condition.

Depression may not qualify as being 'long-term' because it may not last 12 months, and it may not recur. In practice, this means that someone experiencing a first episode of depression may not qualify as disabled, where someone who has had several episodes (which add up to more than 12 months) may.

Depression will only be considered a disability if it has an impact on a person's ability to carry out routine day-to-day tasks – this does not apply to any specialist skills that a person may have, but only to routine tasks that any able person might do as a matter of routine. In practice, depression will be a disability if it impacts on:

⇨ Mobility

⇨ Manual dexterity

⇨ Physical co-ordination

⇨ Continence

⇨ Ability to lift, carry or otherwise move everyday objects

⇨ Speech, hearing or eyesight

⇨ Memory or ability to concentrate, learn or understand

⇨ Perception of the risk of physical danger.

A person's ability/disability is judged according to how they would be without any treatment they might be receiving. So if, for example, you are taking an antidepressant that allows to function, your status would be assessed in terms of how your depression would affect you if you were not taking the antidepressant.

The disclosure dilemma

Because of the discrimination experienced by people with depression, many choose not to disclose their condition or to limit disclosure only to those who have to know. However, non-disclosure can cause problems if at a later stage they need to establish that their condition is severe and enduring. For example, in many cases people do not disclose their depression to a potential employer because they fear that this could count against them. However, if they become depressed later on, their employer may be able to lawfully dismiss them for failing to disclose their condition when they were first employed.

There is currently no solution to the disclosure dilemma. If you do disclose, you may well encounter discrimination. If you don't disclose and are later discriminated against, you may not be protected under the DDA.

Sources of support

You can find out more about your rights on the Equalities and Human Rights Commission website. If you feel that you have been discriminated against, it is important that you seek appropriate advice. There are several potential sources of help:

⇨ Trades Unions offer legal services to their members

⇨ Law Centres operate in many areas, providing free legal advice

⇨ Citizens Advice can offer advice on DDA issues

⇨ Many private law firms specialise in DDA cases – but you should make sure you see a solicitor with experience in disability law.

⇨ The above information is reprinted with kind permission from Journeys Toward Recovery. Please visit www.journeysonline.org.uk for further information.

© Journeys Toward Recovery 2014

Stigma and discrimination

Stigma and discrimination can have a huge impact on the lives of people affected by depression and, for many, they are the single biggest barrier to recovery.

Stigma is experienced by people affected by depression when negative judgements are made about them based on the condition, usually as a result of stereotypes, misconceptions or fear. Stigma can take many forms. It may be someone making an unpleasant remark or ignoring you; or assumptions being made about the kind of person you are or your abilities. Discrimination is the active part of stigma, when someone is not only judged because of the condition they experience but is actually treated differently.

It may seem that understanding and awareness of mental health problems is improving but many studies have shown that stigma is still widespread. Consider the following statistics:

⇨ The most common mental illnesses are anxiety and depression (22% of the population) but when asked to describe mental illness 63% of people said it was 'someone with schizophrenia' (which affects just 1% of the population). This figure has increased from 56% ten years ago (Department of Health 2007).

⇨ The number of people who believe that someone with a mental illness is 'someone who has to be kept in a psychiatric or mental hospital' has also increased over the past decade, from 47% to 59% (Department of Health 2007).

⇨ Belief in the link between mental illness and violence has similarly risen, from 29% to 36% (Department of Health 2007).

⇨ A fifth of employers say that they would not employ someone who had been in receipt of Incapacity Benefit (Chartered Institute for Personnel Development May 2006).

⇨ 18% of employers said that they would not employ someone who has experienced mental ill health compared to 10% who wouldn't employ someone with a physical disability (Chartered Institute for Personnel Development May 2006).

Institutionalised discrimination

Stigma and discrimination start at the top, creating a climate within which employers routinely exclude people with mental health problems from work and other organisations feel empowered to discriminate too.

The state discriminates by:

⇨ Having legislation that allows internment on the grounds of a person's medical condition (as opposed to whether someone is dangerous)

⇨ Giving less weight to witness evidence from people who have had mental illness

⇨ Barring people who have had mental illness from public service – for example, not allowing them to sit on juries

⇨ Barring people who have had mental illness from holding public office

⇨ The Royal College of Psychiatrists has recently drawn attention to a range of health professions whose entry criteria exclude people who have had mental health problems.

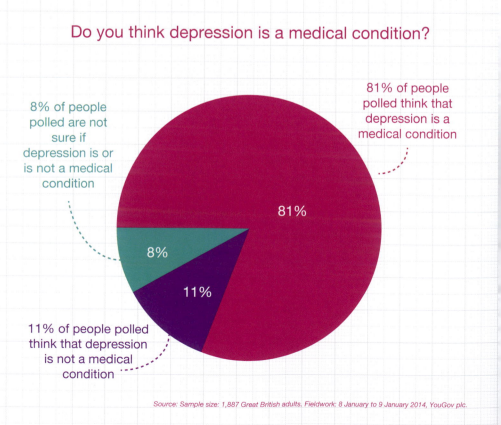

Do you think depression is a medical condition?

8% of people polled are not sure if depression is or is not a medical condition

81% of people polled think that depression is a medical condition

11% of people polled think that depression is not a medical condition

81%

8%

11%

Source: Sample size: 1,887 Great British adults. Fieldwork: 8 January to 9 January 2014, YouGov plc.

⇨ Even where people with mental health problems are not openly excluded, informal discrimination makes it hard for them to pursue a career in professions such as law, medicine and politics – a recent report by the All-Party Parliamentary Group on Mental Health found that one in five Members of Parliament has had mental health problems, but most felt they could not disclose this publicly.

Insurance companies may deny health, personal and holiday insurance to people who have had mental health problems, and can refuse to pay a claim where an applicant failed to disclose their history, even where this has no bearing on the claim.

Employers regularly exclude people with mental health problems from work – seeking to sack those who develop problems while refusing to employ those with a history of mental illness.

Self-exclusion

Another manifestation of discrimination is a process of self-exclusion in which people behave as if discrimination will always happen. For example, while someone with depression is right to fear that they might be discriminated against in employment, they would be wrong to believe this will always be the case. If, however, they avoid seeking employment, and fail to take advantage of the help available because of this fear, it becomes a self-fulfilling prophecy.

Stigma in the media

The media regularly link mental illness with violence and homicide even though the number of homicides by people with a mental illness has fallen significantly over the last 50 years (during which time, the number of homicides has increased by more than 500%).

Elsewhere, the media regularly use stigmatising language on a par with some of the language used to

describe ethnic minorities back in the 1970s.

While challenges can be made against television and radio coverage of mental illness through the regulator Ofcom, the Press Complaints Commission only considers complaints where an individual is directly affected by press coverage. So, for example, only Frank Bruno could complain about the 'Bonkers Bruno' headline – those of us who feel it is inappropriate to use the term 'bonkers' to describe someone with a mental illness have no right of redress. This said, we all have the choice not to buy newspapers and not to subscribe to TV stations that discriminate in this way.

Over-estimating severity

The majority of people with a history of mental illness choose not to disclose their condition publicly – or to be very selective about who they disclose to.

One problem that arises from this is that those people who are 'out' about their mental illness are often those who have little choice in the matter – those with the most severe and enduring conditions; those in long-term contact with

specialist services; those who have been in contact with the criminal justice system; those who have been excluded from employment; those in poor housing; those who lack social networks and intimate relationships.

This leads politicians, health and social care professionals, journalists, voluntary organisations, and user/survivor groups themselves to stigmatise the majority of people with mental illness as being much needier, much more dependent and much less self-resilient than is actually the case, by applying the characteristics of the 10% with the most severe and enduring illness to the 90% with common mental illness.

Many people with depression find it highly stigmatising to be legally categorised as 'vulnerable' or as 'disabled', when most, for most of the time, are fully able to work and to function in society.

⇨ The above information is reprinted with kind permission from Journeys Toward Recovery. Please visit www.journeysonline.org.uk for further information.

© Journeys Toward Recovery 2014

Depression is NOT a mental illness

By Jamie Flexman, guitar teacher, writer and fan of the unconventional

It's physical

This is a short article that I wish to get out there because it constantly irritates me about the many misconceptions regarding depression, what it is and who gets it. I want to begin by asking a simple question.

What is the difference between depression and food poisoning?

I'll tell you.

With food poisoning you can phone in sick to work and your boss will allow you to have a day or two off with no questions asked. Have you ever tried to phone in sick with depression? I bet most of you haven't, mainly because you just KNOW that your boss won't believe you, let alone be OK with it.

So you make up a 'real' illness – you know, one that everyone can relate to

How about when your friend asks you how you are feeling today? With food poisoning you can straight out tell them what is wrong and you will get sympathy in return. Tell them you are feeling down and all you'll probably get is a 'well cheer up, it can't be that bad'.

It's at this point you fantasise about punching them in the face.

The media, bless 'em, do their best to paint any form of mental illness in a positive light. Explaining that depression, anxiety, addiction and anything related to those three are now legitimate diseases that deserve the same respect and attention as anything physical.

Well thanks but the last I heard, the brain was a part of the body, and a damn important one at that.

As long as we treat an illness of the brain as something different from the rest of the body then it will never receive the same amount of attention.

Unless you have experienced it, you can never truly understand

How many of you have a tail? You know, like a monkey. If you haven't (which I hope is everyone), can you imagine what it is like to grip a branch or maybe just swing it back and forth? It's impossible isn't it?

We've never had one so that's not surprising.

Depression is similar to that. If it's something that you have never experienced then you can try as hard as you want, but you will never truly know what it feels like.

Are you having a bad day? Nope that's not depression.

Are you bummed out because that girl/guy you like has just rejected your advances? Nope that's not depression.

Have you spent all week in a foul mood because your favourite team has lost a cup final? Nope that's not depression either.

It isn't a change in mood related to a trivial life event. If your whole world is slowly being turned upside down because of what is happening inside your mind then you may well be depressed. If these thoughts have been present for several weeks or months then yes, you may be depressed.

There is a big difference between feeling down and having depression and this brings me to my next point.

You cannot just 'snap out of it' or 'pull yourself together'

I like analogies so steady your hats because here comes another one.

Depression is like trying to run through water and being told to get over it is akin to suddenly being able to move like you can on dry land. It's impossible. You can grit your teeth and attempt to get some momentum going but ultimately the density will prevent you from moving quickly.

When depression has its grip on you, life becomes water. The air around you becomes water, crushing you with its weight and even the simplest tasks become difficult. You feel sluggish, both mentally and physically and nothing can snap you out of it.

You have essentially become trapped inside your own prison and true access to your brain lies behind that locked door. Sometimes, briefly, you are allowed outside to stretch your legs but you know this is temporary. Eventually you will have to return to your cell and wait patiently for a time when you are given another opportunity to function like a normal member of society.

There is no choice in the matter. All we can do is take advantage of our good days and try to minimise the effect our bad days have on us.

Here is what I want you to do

If you have ever experienced any form of depression, anxiety or addiction then please share this article via your social media. The more people that understand, the less stressful and easier our lives will become.

17 September 2013

⇨ The above information is reprinted with kind permission from Jamie Flexman. Please visit www.psycholocrazy.com for further information.

© Jamie Flexman 2014

Glenn Close: 'I feel shame I didn't pay attention to my bipolar sister'

In London to promote a mental health initiative, Glenn Close reveals the challenges her own family is facing.

By Celia Walden

'When my sister, Jessie, was seven,' Glenn Close recalls, 'she would rub a finger between her thumb and forefinger until it was raw and crusty. She would keep on rubbing until she was in pain. Looking back, that should have been an indication that something was going on.'

That something turned out to be bipolar 1 disorder, also known as manic depression, which causes serious shifts in mood, energy and behaviour. Close's younger sister was diagnosed at the age of 47. 'Jessie said to me one day: "I can't stop thinking about killing myself. I need help."' It was a tragedy, Close reflects sadly, that she wasn't diagnosed before then. 'But nobody in our family had a clue. I feel a real sense of shame that I didn't pay more attention at the time.'

It is to spare other families that heartache and shame – a word Close feels is too often associated with mental illness – that the 66-year-old, six-time Oscar-nominated star of *Fatal Attraction* and *Dangerous Liaisons* founded the anti-stigma campaign, Bring Change 2 Mind, in 2009. Boosted by the famous faces who've gone public on their mental health issues – Ruby Wax, Stephen Fry, Catherine Zeta-Jones and Oprah Winfrey, who this week spoke of a recent nervous breakdown – Close and Jessie, now 56, have been engaged in a campaign of stigma-busting ever since.

Along with Jessie's son, Calen, who suffers from schizoaffective disorder, characterised by disordered thought processes and abnormal emotional responses, their methods include speaking engagements, TV public service announcements and a hard-hitting advert, *Schizo: The Movie*. Last week, they joined forces in London with Time to Change – a British programme that challenges mental health discrimination – for a global meeting of like-minded campaigners.

Jessie is the youngest of the four Close children, who grew up in Greenwich, Connecticut. Their father was a surgeon who became involved in an extreme conservative missionary movement, Moral Re-Armament, and he and their mother were absent for long stretches. 'Nobody was consistently around to watch what Jessie was going through,' Close has said.

Jessie left school in ninth grade, married at 16 and got pregnant soon after. 'All of those things were signs, of course,' Close tells me. 'But back then her behaviour was called "acting out", "rebelling" or "being perverse".' Even after her sister's first suicide attempt, at 16, the actress admits that she 'just didn't put two and two together'.

'Then Jessie married somebody she never should have married and was living in LA. That was when the second suicide attempt happened. We were horrified. At that point, my mother and I went to rescue her.' Despite the following years of alcoholism and depression, the idea that Jessie might be suffering from a mental illness was never considered. It wasn't until 2001 and her third suicide attempt – which this time involved a gun – that Jessie sought help, first through AA, and then at the McLean hospital in Massachusetts, where Calen had been in treatment for two years.

'That was where they finally diagnosed her. But you know what?' Close says with a mirthless laugh. 'I still heard my parents wondering whether she "enjoyed" being mentally ill.'

Today, Close is intent on breaking down such prejudice. 'People believe that those with mental illnesses are frightening. They don't want them living next to them or dating their son or daughter. They don't want them teaching their child and they don't want them in the workplace.'

Although strides have been made over the past decade – in February a Mental Health Discrimination Bill was passed in the UK that put an end to laws preventing people with mental health problems from carrying out jury service or becoming a company director – Close believes that the stigma remains.

Ask the actress how we go about changing that, and her measured tones become more dynamic. 'That's the huge challenge. The best way for a person to change their behaviour towards mental illness is to meet someone who is suffering from one.

'When my nephew, Calen, wanted to date Meg – now his wife – she had to tell her parents that a boy with schizoaffective disorder wanted to ask her out. Initially they were horrified. Then they met him,' she smiles. 'But how do you get that one-on-one effect with whole populations? We need to keep reminding ourselves that we are not our illnesses. If we had cancer or diabetes, we wouldn't be defined by that, would we? But it's ultimately about ignorance – and fear.

'We need to be able to say out loud all the various disorders of mental illness and understand them. "Schizophrenia" is a very frightening word. So is "bipolar" or "depression", even.'

Hollywood does little to reassure the public on the subject of mental health, sensationalising it to gain higher audience figures. Last June, Close made headlines when she said that she regretted feeding the stigma by playing Alex Forrest, the unstable, homicidal anti-heroine of the 1980s hit, *Fatal Attraction*.

She spoke to two psychiatrists when preparing for the role. 'What seems odd is that mental illness was never mentioned,' she says now. 'In fact, the ending was changed to turn Alex into a psychopath, when really she wasn't one. She was more self-destructive. That is something that Hollywood does for plot reasons, and it was probably the reason the movie became such a hit, because the disturbing person was removed in the end.

'It catered to the cliché of what we do when somebody is mentally ill: we remove them.' She adds sarcastically: 'Because, of course, they all become violent. Hollywood always has to find a protagonist or an antagonist, and either it's a Nazi or a Taliban leader or a psychopath.'

But wouldn't it be dangerous to avoid representing the mentally ill altogether?

'Absolutely,' she says. 'But it might be interesting to explain a little bit more about it. In *Fatal Attraction*, Alex had this weird relationship with her father that was never explained. One psychiatrist told me that the character had been a victim of incest at an early age, which might have triggered all the psychological difficulties she went through.'

Hollywood aside, Close's mission becomes more challenging every time a mentally ill loner is violent in real life. This happens all too frequently in America. In December, Adam Lanza killed 20 schoolchildren and six staff members at Sandy Hook Elementary School. Last week, Aaron Alexis killed 12 people at Washington Navy Yard. Both were said to have suffered from mental health issues.

'I've been told that [Alexis] did try to reach out to people and had been hearing voices,' says Close. 'That should be a red flag. That somebody who is hearing voices still has that security clearance… Somebody should have gone to the nearest mental health office and said: "This man needs help."

'Hopefully, we will come to a point where people who are a danger will be spotted before it's too late. We have to take care of our own. It's imperative that our family doctors are educated about mental illness and that friends and families understand that it's something they should be open about.'

A Mental Health Discrimination Bill was passed in the UK that put an end to laws preventing people with mental health problems from carrying out jury service or becoming a company director

Things may be better for Glenn and her family now, but daily life is still an exercise in caution. 'We've learnt to have antennae out for changes of season when [Jessie] can get manic or depressed. We listen for changes in her voice, and we know what sort of a medication schedule she needs. It's about learning to live with chronic illness.'

And her nephew, Calen? 'He's a different person; he just blows me away. He recently told me, "I had to figure out what was clarity and what wasn't",' and here there's the smallest crack in Close's voice. "Then I would cling to those moments of clarity until more would come – and still more. Now, after 11 years, I finally feel like my brain is healing."'

Find out more and watch 'Schizo: the Movie' at time-to-change.org. uk and visit Glenn Close's project at www.bringchange2mind.org.

23 September 2013

⇨ The above information is reprinted with kind permission from *The Telegraph*. Please visit www.telegraph.co.uk for further information.

Five ways to tackle SAD

From nutrition to naturopathy, five experts tell you how to beat the winter blues.

By Patsy Westcott

Professor Anne Farmer, consultant psychiatrist

'Half an hour to an hour under a 10,000 lux "daylight lamp" every morning from September or October to March or April, can really help, especially for people who are "larks" who are usually brighter first thing in the morning.

'"Owls", people who perk up at night may find early evening more helpful. It's important to stay under the lamp for the required length of time and not to keep getting up and down.

'Antidepressants can help some either with light therapy or on their own. Depending on severity I might also prescribe Prozac or another SSRI.

'A serotonin and noradrenaline reuptake inhibitor such as venlafaxine, a drug that creates both more of both hormones can help increase alertness and energy as well as tackling the depression.'

Marilyn Glenville, nutritional therapist

'An underactive thyroid can up the risk of depression and women are prone to this, especially as they get older so I'd encourage patients to get a thyroid test.

'Peaks and dips in blood sugar can exacerbate symptoms so I would advise cutting out caffeine, and unrefined foods like white bread, biscuits, pastries and cakes. I advise them to eat little and often.

'Chromium, found in foods like seafood, liver and fresh fruit and vegetables, helps combat carb cravings, which are a feature of winter depression. B complex vitamins found in foods such as oats, barley, avocado, salmon and Brazil nuts can help balance the nerves.

'I would also recommend supplements: a good multi-vitamin and mineral plus 25 mg of B complex vitamins, 1,000 mg of Omega 3s and 100 mcg of chromium which helps reduce sugar cravings.

'Exercise is an essential part of the plan – I would suggest going out for a brisk half hour walk at the lightest time of day.'

Linda Blair, psychotherapist

'Cognitive behaviour therapy doesn't take away the symptoms of SAD but it can help patients to accept and manage them better.

'When you learn how to see SAD as just a part of your life it gives you choices. I would recommend behavioural changes such as using a daylight alarm clock that emits increasing light levels to simulate the arrival of dawn as you gradually wake up and regular aerobic exercise to encourage the body to produce endorphins, its own feel-good hormones.

'It is important to give yourself the chance to cut down on stress at this time of year, so I would advise putting a sticker in your diary to remind you to go easier on yourself.

'It's a good idea to make a list of things that make you feel better, such as phoning a friend or relative and keeping this in several different places, so you have a kind of mental toolkit to call on when you feel down. And of course if you can afford it take a holiday somewhere sunny.'

Penny Povey, naturopath

'A good diet is vital. Start the day with porridge. For lunch I would advise a bowl of vegetable soup or big salad with fish or turkey; for supper eat a handful of protein – again things like fish and turkey – and some complex carbohydrates that help calm anxiety, something like brown rice and cooked veg. It's important to get some exercise – and fresh air.

'Herbs can be useful as an alternative to antidepressants. Licorice helps tonify the adrenal glands, which are often involved in depression. Oat straw is also good for the nervous system. St John's Wort is good for mild to moderate depression and the herb Rodeola can help combat stress. Siberian ginseng helps to strengthen the adrenals and balances the system generally.'

Phil Edmonds, registered homeopath

'The homeopathic remedy sepia can be good for depression that is made better by the sun, especially when the person is feeling overwhelmed, overworked and alone.

'Pulsatilla can help when the person is weepy and emotional but feels better when comforted. Nat Mur is good for grief that is linked to the past, while for really severe cases I might choose Aurum, especially for people who are perfectionists.'

Winter warmers

To help get you through the long winter nights here are some nutritious meal ideas.

- ⇨ Pot-au-feu
- ⇨ Onion and thyme soup with brie croutons
- ⇨ Sausages with peppery bubble and squeak
- ⇨ Low fat lamb stew on the quick
- ⇨ Oxtail stew with cinnamon and star anise
- ⇨ Spiced parsnip soup
- ⇨ Ribollita, a Tuscan bean soup

- ⇨ The above information is reprinted with kind permission from Saga Magazine. Please visit www.saga.co.uk/magazine for further information.

© Saga Magazine 2014

Postnatal depression

Postnatal depression is very common, affecting at least one in ten new mothers and one in 14 fathers, but many can suffer in silence because their condition is not recognised or dismissed as simply the 'baby blues'. Postnatal depression is an illness, and although it is not known for certain what causes it, some experts believe that the sudden change in hormones after the birth may trigger the condition. Getting postnatal depression is not failing and nor is it related to how capable a person is, it is an illness.

When does postnatal depression develop?

It usually develops within the first four to six weeks, but can start even several months following childbirth and can emerge at any time during the first year. It comes on either gradually or all of a sudden, and can range from being relatively mild to hard-hitting. Postnatal depression is still an illness that is not widely understood by mums who experience it or by their family and friends. In fact, it is often viewed with shame by sufferers who may feel a "failure" or a "bad mother" because they feel unable to cope. In fact, the opposite is true, with all the evidence showing that mothers with postnatal illness are at least as good at mothering as those without.

Postnatal depression symptoms

⇨ Crying a lot, often over the smallest things

⇨ Poor concentration

⇨ Anxiety

⇨ Guilt

⇨ Lack of confidence in your ability as a mother or father

⇨ Not enjoying being a parent

⇨ Loss of appetite or overeating

⇨ Extreme tiredness

⇨ Irritability

⇨ Fear of harming the baby, though the reality is that only in very rare cases is anyone harmed

⇨ Sleeping problems

⇨ No interest in sex

⇨ Being hostile or indifferent to your husband or partner

⇨ A sense of being overwhelmed and unable to cope

⇨ Difficulty in making decisions or concentrating

⇨ Physical symptoms, such as stomach pains, headaches and blurred vision

How is postnatal depression diagnosed?

Postnatal depression is usually diagnosed by a doctor based on what those who know you, tell him or her. Sometimes the doctor may do a blood test to rule out physical reasons for the symptoms, such as anaemia. A short questionnaire has been developed called the Edinburgh Postnatal Depression Scale and has ten simple questions. Doctors and health visitors may ask a patient to fill it in if they suspect postnatal depression.

Postnatal depression treatments

The most important thing you can do for yourself is believe that you will get better.

Try to get as much rest as you can, although this can be difficult with a small baby. Try to recruit the help of friends or family and readily accept any offers of help that come along. This is very important, as tiredness seems to make depression worse.

Don't try to force yourself back to normal too quickly. Many mothers feel that by keeping busy such as going back to work, things will right themselves, but this can actually prolong the illness.

Be kind to yourself. Don't force yourself to do things you don't really want to do or that upset you.

Exercise. It can be difficult to be active when all you want to do is curl up and go to sleep but exercise releases endorphins.

Possible sources of help include the GP, midwife, health visitor, community psychiatric nurse, psychotherapist, counsellor or psychiatrist. Experts suggest that the best treatment for postnatal depression may be a combination of practical support and advice, psychotherapy, counselling and, if necessary, antidepressants.

Support and advice

Support and understanding from friends and relatives can help recovery and it is far better to talk about your feelings rather than bottling them up. Ask your health visitor about what is available in the area, such as self-help

Postnatal depression in new parents

One in ten new mothers are affected by postnatal depression.

One in fourteen new fathers are affected by postnatal depression.

Source: Postnatal depression, 2014, Family Lives.

or support groups which can provide lots of encouragement and advice.

Counselling

These treatments can be very effective and offer you the opportunity to explore any underlying factors that could have contributed to the postnatal depression. Although the availability of counselling can depend on where you live, many GPs now have a counsellor or psychotherapist attached to their surgery. They can also refer to a psychologist or psychiatrist on the NHS.

Antidepressants

Many mothers, particularly those with milder symptoms, recover without antidepressants, but they can be very effective for postnatal depression. A GP can prescribe different kinds of medication to help and it is important to discuss all the options fully beforehand. They can take a month or two to start working effectively, although if you don't feel any benefits during that time, see your doctor again and he or she may need to try a different drug or adjust the medication. It's also important to remember that any medication can enter the breast milk and this will be a major consideration.

⇨ The above information is reprinted with kind permission from Family Lives. Please visit www.familylives.org.uk for further information.

Computer light at night 'causes depression', study suggests

Exposure to light at night – even from a tablet or laptop computer – may cause depression, according to a new study.

Researchers have found that exposure to bright light elevates levels of a stress hormone in the body which triggers depression and reduces the ability to learn.

Up until the invention of electricity, humans rose with the sun and slept when it set. However, people can now continue to work into the early hours.

The new study of mice found this may come at a serious cost. When people routinely work late, they risk suffering depression and learning problems, and not only because of lack of sleep. The culprit could also be exposure to light at night from lamps, computers and even iPads.

Samer Hattar, a biology professor at Johns Hopkins University in the United States, said: 'Basically, what we found is that chronic exposure to bright light – even the kind of light you experience in your own living room at home or in the workplace at night if you are a shift worker – elevates levels of a certain stress hormone in the body, which results in depression and lowers cognitive function.'

The study demonstrates how cells in the eye – called intrinsically photosensitive retinal ganglion cells – are activated by bright light, affecting the brain's centre for mood, memory and learning.

Prof. Hattar added: 'Mice and humans are actually very much alike in many ways, and one similarity is that they have these cells in their eyes which affect them the same way.'

The scientists knew that shorter days in the winter cause some people to develop a form of depression known as seasonal affective disorder (SAD) and that some patients with the mood disorder benefit from light therapy, which is regular exposure to bright light.

Prof. Hattar's team believed that mice would react in the same way, and tested their theory by exposing laboratory rodents to a cycle consisting of 3.5 hours of light and then 3.5 hours of darkness. Previous studies using this cycle showed that it did not disrupt the mice's sleep cycles, but the team found that it did cause the animals to develop depression-like behaviours.

Prof. Hattar said: 'Of course, you can't ask mice how they feel, but we did see an increase in depression-like behaviours, including a lack of interest in sugar or pleasure-seeking, and the study mice moved around far less during some of the tests we did.

'They also clearly did not learn as quickly or remember tasks as well. They were not as interested in novel objects as were mice on a regular light-darkness cycle schedule.'

He said the animals also had increased levels of cortisol, a stress hormone that has been linked in numerous previous studies with learning issues.

Treatment with Prozac, a commonly prescribed antidepressant, mitigated the symptoms, restoring the mice to their previous healthy moods and levels of learning, and bolstering the evidence that their learning issues were caused by depression.

Prof. Hattar said the results indicate that humans should be wary of the kind of prolonged, regular exposure to bright light at night.

'I'm not saying we have to sit in complete darkness at night, but I do recommend that we should switch on fewer lamps, and stick to less-intense light bulbs,' he said.

The findings were published in the journal *Nature*.

24 February 2014

⇨ The above information is reprinted with kind permission from *The Scotsman*. Please visit www.scotsman.com for further information.

Scientists find revolutionary 'biomarker' for clinical depression in teenage boys

Young men who have depressive symptoms and high cortisol levels are the most susceptible.

By Emily Dugan

A revolutionary way of identifying the teenage boys who are most likely to develop clinical depression in later life has been discovered by researchers at the University of Cambridge.

Predicting those who may be at risk of depressive symptoms has been puzzling doctors for decades but now scientists have found the first biomarker – or biological signpost – for clinical depression.

Teenage boys who have a combination of depressive symptoms and raised levels of the stress hormone cortisol are up to 14 times more likely to develop clinical depression than those who show neither trait.

'The prospect of identifying boys at risk at an earlier stage, should enable us to make a big step forward in successfully treating serious mental illness'

Around one in six people suffer from clinical depression at some point in their lives and three-quarters of mental health diseases start before people are 24 years old. Researchers believe this latest discovery, published last night in the journal *Proceedings of the National Academy of Sciences of the United States of America* (*PNAS*), could help target treatment and mean doctors can intervene earlier.

Professor Ian Goodyer from the University of Cambridge, who led the study, said: 'Depression is a terrible illness that will affect as many as ten million people in the UK at some point in their lives. Through our research, we now have a very real way of identifying those teenage boys most likely to develop clinical depression.

'This will help us strategically target preventions and interventions at these individuals and hopefully help to reduce their risk of serious episodes of depression and their consequences in adult life.'

At the moment the indicators work only for men because cortisol levels are higher in women and they have not found an equivalent way of predicting outcomes for female patients.

Researchers analysed several early morning saliva samples taken within a week from more than 1,850 teenagers – and did the same again a year later. The samples showed cortisol levels were stable over the year and were then combined with self-reports about symptoms of depression.

The teenagers were then divided into four groups, ranging from group one, who had normal levels of morning cortisol and low symptoms of depression over time, through to group four, who had elevated levels of morning cortisol and high symptoms of depression over time.

Teenage boys in group four were 14 times more likely to develop clinical depression than those in the first group.

Teenage girls in this fourth group were only four times more likely than those in the first group to develop major depression – and were no more likely to develop the condition than those with either high morning cortisol or symptoms of depression alone. The findings suggest gender differences in how depression develops.

Paul Jenkins, chief executive of Rethink Mental Illness, said: 'These findings represent a major development in our understanding of depression among teenage boys. When young people receive early intervention treatment, they have a much better chance of getting better and avoiding long-term mental health problems.

'Around one in six people suffer from clinical depression at some point in their lives and three-quarters of mental health diseases start before people are 24 years old'

'The prospect of identifying boys at risk at an earlier stage, should enable us to make a big step forward in successfully treating serious mental illness.'

John Williams, head of neuroscience and mental health at the Wellcome Trust, which funded the research, said: 'Progress in identifying biological markers for depression has been frustratingly slow, but now we finally have a biomarker for clinical depression. The approach taken by Professor Goodyer's team may yet yield further biomarkers. It also gives tantalising clues about the gender differences in the causes and onset of depression.'

17 February 2014

⇨ The above information is reprinted with kind permission from *The Independent*. Please visit www.indepedent.co.uk for further information.

© 2014 independent.co.uk

Mental health warning for jobless young

The Prince's Trust Macquarie Youth Index has found that more than three quarters of a million young people believe they have nothing to live for, with jobless youngsters facing 'devastating' symptoms of mental illness.

The research reveals that long-term unemployed young people are more than twice as likely as their peers to have been prescribed antidepressants. One in three have contemplated suicide, while one in four have self-harmed.

The findings are based on interviews with 2,161 16-to-25-year-olds and show that 40 per cent of jobless young people have faced these symptoms of mental illness – including suicidal thoughts, feelings of self-loathing and panic attacks – as a direct result of unemployment.

Long-term unemployed young people are also more than twice as likely as their peers to believe they have nothing to live for.

The Prince's Trust is now calling for urgent support from government, health agencies and employers to fund its vital work with long-term unemployed young people battling mental health issues. With more support the youth charity can help more young people build their self-esteem and move into work.

Martina Milburn, chief executive of youth charity The Prince's Trust, said: 'Unemployment is proven to cause devastating, long-lasting mental health problems among young people. Thousands wake up every day believing that life isn't worth living, after struggling for years in the dole queue.

The sixth annual Youth Index – which gauges young people's well-being across a range of areas from family life to physical health – highlights that unemployed young people are significantly less likely to ask for help if they are struggling to cope. Three quarters of long-term unemployed young people do not have someone to confide in.

David Fass, CEO of Macquarie Group, EMEA, said: 'Macquarie invests in young people. We think it's important to identify the key issues they face today so policy and programmes aimed at addressing them can be developed. The Index enables organisations like The Prince's Trust to offer disadvantaged young people the guidance they need to build a stronger future and Macquarie hopes these findings will help further target the support available.'

Shirley Cramer CBE, chief executive of the Royal Society for Public Health, said:

'This research proves that unemployment is a public health issue. It is one that must be tackled urgently and it is essential that youth unemployment is added to the public health agenda.'

She went on to say, 'Unemployed young people are struggling in many aspects of their lives, from their mental health and well-being to their relationships and their qualifications and we must act quickly to end this.'

In response to these findings, The Prince's Trust is increasing support for the UK's most vulnerable young people through its Get Started programme which aims to inspire and motivate the long-term unemployed.

The Prince's Trust 'Get Started' courses are run in partnership with organisations such as the Premier League, the PFA, ASOS and Sony Computer Entertainment Europe, reaching thousands more of the country's hardest-to-reach young people over the next three years.

This year, The Prince's Trust will support 58,000 disadvantaged young people, helping them turn their lives around. Three in four young people supported by The Prince's Trust move into work, education or training.

⇨ The above information is reprinted with kind permission from The Prince's Trust. Please visit www.princes-trust.org.uk for further information.

© 2014 The Prince's Trust

Symptom	All young people	Long-term unemployment
I have been prescribed antidepressants	11%	26%
I have experienced panic attacks	22%	29%
I have experienced insomnia (have trouble sleeping)	37%	39%
I have felt suicidal	26%	32%
I have self-harmed	19%	24%
I have had difficulty controlling my anger	20%	25%
I take drugs	8%	12%

THE CONVERSATION

Half of teens outgrow depression and anxiety

An article from The Conversation.

By Fron Jackson-Webb, Senior Editor at The Conversation

Around half of teens who experience a brief episode of depression or anxiety do not go on to have a mental illness in adulthood, according to a study from the Murdoch Children's Research Institute.

Half of girls and almost one-third of boys have an episode of depression or anxiety in their teens but rates drop sharply when young people reach their 20s.

The study is published today in *The Lancet* medical journal.

The researchers followed more than 1,900 adolescents from 1992 to 2008, assessing them for mental disorders at five points during adolescence and three in young adulthood.

The study defined depression and anxiety as a 'level at which a family doctor would be concerned'.

'The good news is teen problems are not a life sentence,' said lead author Professor George Patton. 'Many of these problems, particularly if they're brief and last for six months or less, or in boys, tend to get better.'

This might be the result of adolescent development, including maturation of the brain systems involved in social and emotional processing, and learning new cognitive and emotional skills.

'Or it could be that young people are successfully transitioning into young adulthood: completing education, leaving home, and developing relationships. 'These things might be kicking in and making a positive difference in their lives,' Professor Patton said.

Yet, reaching your 20s without problems is not a guarantee against mental health problems. Almost one in five participants had their first episodes in their 20s, suggesting the risk period for onset of depression and anxiety problems extends into young adulthood.

Professor Louise Newman, Director of the Centre for Developmental Psychiatry and Psychology at Monash University, said the study was well conducted and gave an accurate picture of the prevalence of mental illness among young Australians.

'Because it's an epidemiological study, it raises some tantalising questions about how we can better understand the risk factors for mental illness,' said Professor Newman.

Professor Newman pointed out however that the study didn't

distinguish between different types of depression and issues related to personality development, which 'in the real world, overlap'.

'The most often-given treatment would be antidepressants and not much else. And that's not the right treatment for adolescents'

She said it was interesting the researchers found an association with parental separation and divorce, and episodes of mental illness among adolescents, which suggests social contexts impact vulnerability.

Treatment

The study authors suggest that early interventions which shorten the duration of episodes of depression and anxiety could help prevent much mental illness later in life.

'If things are not getting better and have been continuing for months, that is the kind of situation where seeking help from a GP, a trained counsellor or psychologist, or an organisation like Headspace would make sense,' said Professor Patton.

'But for many of these kids, they will get over these problems. In this instance, the intervention we're talking about is not an intervention with medication or even formal psychotherapy, it's about allowing the young person to talk about the problems in their life and come to solutions that work for them', he said.

University of Adelaide professor of psychiatry Jon Jureidini warned that benefits of medical therapies for depression were often over-stated.

'It's always assumed that treating depression will improve those outcomes in the long term but there's no evidence to support that,' Professor Jureidini said.

'The most often-given treatment would be antidepressants and not much else. And that's not the right treatment for depressed adolescents.

Symptoms of anxiety

Generalised anxiety disorder (GAD) can affect you physically and mentally. How severe they are varies from person to person.

Psychological symptoms of anxiety

GAD can cause a change in a persons behaviour and the way they think and feel about things. Psychological symptoms of GAD include:

- restlessness
- a sense of dread
- feeling constantly 'on edge'
- difficulty concentrating
- irritability
- impatience
- being easily distracted.

These symptoms may cause a person to withdraw from social contact (seeing family and friends) to avoid feelings of worry and dread. They may also find going to work difficult and stressful and may take time off sick. These actions can cause more worry and increase a person's lack of self-esteem.

Physical symptoms of anxiety

The physical symptoms of GAD can include:

- dizziness
- drowsiness and tiredness
- pins and needles
- irregular heartbeat (palpitations)
- muscle aches and tension
- dry mouth
- excessive sweating
- shortness of breath
- stomach ache
- difficulty falling or staying asleep (insomnia) .

Source: NHS Choices 2012

'The right treatment for depressed adolescents is to try to understand what's going on for the person. Depression is not a description, not an explanation.

'We should never ignore young people's distress but taking it seriously doesn't mean we need to treat it – there might be other responses to it.'

Child and adolescent psychiatrist Dr Peter Parry agreed, saying it was important to be wary of biological explanations for adolescent emotions.

'It reads as a very good epidemiological study but with nearly half of males and two-thirds of females having at least one episode of clinical anxiety or depressive disorder, we are almost talking about universal human experience,' he said.

'Another aspect is that anxiety and grief are normal mammalian responses to loss and stress. Not all suffering is abnormal – the context always matters – though help in normal suffering is still often needed and can lead to increased insight, maturer coping strategies and resilience.'

16 January 2014

- The above information is reprinted with kind permission from The Conversation. Please visit www.theconversation.com for further information.

© 2010-2014, The Conversation Trust (UK)

Negative effects of social networking

Over a third (34%) of young people have felt depressed because of something they have seen on a social network site and one in seven (14%) have been victims of cyberbullying, according to a YouGov survey commissioned by The Prince's Trust.

By Cordelia Nelson in Life and Social Media

34% of 16–25-year-olds in the UK say they have felt depressed as a direct result of something they have viewed on a social networking website. Young women are more likely to be negatively affected by posts they have seen on social networks.

⇨ More than a third (34%) of young people in Britain have felt depressed because of something they have seen on a social network site, compared to 44% who disagree with this

⇨ Almost one in four (39%) women aged between 16 and 25 have felt miserable as a direct result of posts they have viewed on social networks, while 30% of young men say the same.

Online bullying

More than one in seven (14%) young Brits also admit that they have been bullied online, with 20% saying that they have witnessed more bullying online than in person. 16–18-year-olds are the most likely to have been victims of cyberbullying and have seen more bullying over the Internet than in real life.

⇨ 14% of 16–25-year-olds say they have been bullied online, while almost seven in ten (69%) disagree with this

⇨ Nearly one in five (18%) Brits aged between 16 and 18 have been victims of cyberbullying, compared to 15% of 19–21-year-olds and 10% of 22–25-year-olds

⇨ 20% of young adults say they have witnessed more bullying online than in person, but over half (53%) disagree with this

⇨ Over three in ten (31%) 16–18-year-olds have seen more cyberbullying than bullying in real life, while only 18% of those aged between 19 and 21 and 14% of 22–25-year-olds say the same.

Internet pals

The poll also reveals that 39% of young adults are friends with people online that they have never met before, which increases to almost half (46%) of 16–18-year-olds.

⇨ Almost four in ten (39%) Brits aged 16–25 say they have made friends with people over the Internet that they have never met, while 46% disagree with this

⇨ A plurality (46%) of 16–18-year-olds say that they are friends with people online that they do not know in person, compared to 39% of 19–21-year-olds and 35% of Brits aged between 22 and 25.

The Prince's Trust helps disadvantaged young people to get their lives on track by supporting 13 to 30-year-olds who are unemployed and those struggling at school and at risk of exclusion

4 January 2013

⇨ The above information is reprinted with kind permission from YouGov. Please visit www.yougov.co.uk for further information.

© 2000-2014 YouGov plc

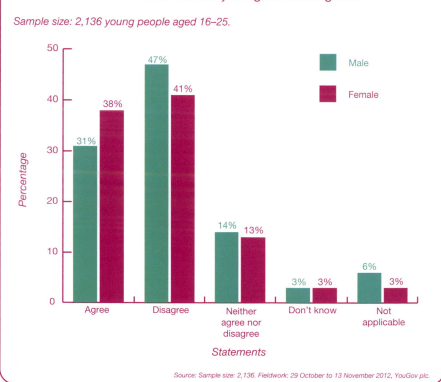

'I have felt depressed as a direct result of something I've seen on a social network.' To what extent do you agree or disagree?

Sample size: 2,136 young people aged 16–25.

Source: Sample size: 2,136. Fieldwork: 29 October to 13 November 2012, YouGov plc.

Antidepressants

Antidepressants are a type of medication used to treat depression or prevent it recurring.

Introduction

Antidepressants are a type of medication used to treat depression or prevent it recurring.

They can also be used to treat a number of other conditions, including:

⇨ obsessive-compulsive disorder (OCD)

⇨ generalised anxiety disorder (GAD)

⇨ post-traumatic stress disorder (PTSD).

Antidepressants are also sometimes used to treat people with long-term (chronic) pain.

How antidepressants work

It is thought antidepressants work by increasing levels of a group of chemicals in the brain called neurotransmitters. Certain neurotransmitters, such as serotonin and noradrenaline, can improve mood and emotion, although this process is not fully understood.

Increasing levels of neurotransmitters can also disrupt pain signals sent by nerves, which may explain why some antidepressants can help relieve long-term pain.

While antidepressants can help treat the symptoms of depression, they do not always address its causes. This is why they are usually used in combination with therapy to treat more severe depression or other mental health conditions caused by emotional distress.

How effective are antidepressants?

Most people benefit from taking antidepressants to some degree, but research suggests that antidepressants may not be as effective as previously thought in cases of mild depression.

However, they are the most effective treatment in relieving symptoms quickly, particularly in cases of severe depression.

The Royal College of Psychiatrists estimates that 50–65% of people treated with an antidepressant for depression will see an improvement, compared to 25–30% of those taking inactive 'dummy' pills (placebos). This means that most people do benefit from antidepressants, even if it is

sometimes a result of the placebo effect.

Doses and duration of treatment

Antidepressants are usually taken in tablet form. When they are prescribed, you will start on the lowest possible dose thought necessary to improve your symptoms.

Antidepressants usually need to be taken for 2–4 weeks (without missing a dose) before the benefit is felt. It's important not to stop taking them because you get some mild side effects early on, as these effects will usually wear off quickly.

If you take an antidepressant for 4–6 weeks without feeling any benefit, speak to your GP or mental health specialist. They may recommend increasing your dose or trying an alternative medication.

A course of treatment usually lasts for six months, although a two-year course may be recommended for people with a previous history of depression and some people with recurrent depression may be advised to take them indefinitely.

Side effects

Different antidepressants can have a range of different side effects. Always check the information leaflet that comes with your medication to see what the possible side effects are. Common side effects of antidepressants in general are usually mild and can include:

⇨ feeling sick

⇨ dry mouth

⇨ slight blurring of vision

⇨ constipation

⇨ dizziness

⇨ drowsiness

⇨ problems sleeping (insomnia)

⇨ sexual dysfunction, such as erectile dysfunction in men or difficulty achieving orgasm.

Side effects should improve within a few days or weeks of treatment as the body gets used to the medication.

Different types of antidepressants

There are a number of different types of antidepressants. Some of the most widely used types are discussed below.

Selective serotonin reuptake inhibitors (SSRIs)

SSRIs are the most widely prescribed type of antidepressants. They are usually preferred over other antidepressants as they cause fewer side effects. An overdose is also less likely to be serious.

Fluoxetine is probably the best known SSRI (sold under the brand name Prozac). Other SSRIs include citalopram (Cipramil), paroxetine (Seroxat) and sertraline (Lustral).

Serotonin-adrenaline reuptake inhibitors (SNRIs)

SNRIs are similar to SSRIs. They were designed to be a more effective antidepressant than SSRIs. However, the evidence that SNRIs are more effective in treating depression is uncertain. It seems some people respond better to SSRIs while others respond better to SNRIs.

Examples of SNRIs include duloxetine (Cymbalta and Yentreve) and venlafaxine (Efexor).

Tricyclic antidepressants (TCAs)

Tricyclic antidepressants (TCAs) are an older type of antidepressant. They are no longer usually recommended as a first-line treatment for depression because they can be more dangerous if an overdose is taken. They also cause more unpleasant side effects than SSRIs and SNRIs.

Exceptions are sometimes made in people with severe depression that fail to respond to other treatments. TCAs may also be recommended for other mental health conditions such as obsessive compulsive disorder and bipolar disorder.

Examples of TCAs include amitriptyline (Tryptizol), clomipramine (Anafranil), imipramine (Tofranil), lofepramine (Gamanil) and nortriptyline (Allegron).

Some types of TCAs, such as amitriptyline, can also be used to treat chronic nerve pain.

Monoamine oxidase inhibitors (MAOIs)

Monoamine oxidase inhibitors (MAOIs) are another older type of antidepressant with a wide range of side effects that are rarely used nowadays. They tend only to be used if other types of antidepressants are not effective and should only be taken under the supervision of a psychiatrist.

A significant drawback of MAOIs is the need to avoid certain foods and drinks, such as cheese and pickled fish, which contain a protein called tyramine. This is because consuming tyramine while taking MAOIs can cause a dangerous rise in blood pressure.

Examples of MAOIs include moclobemide (Manerix) and phenelzine (Nardil).

Alternatives to antidepressants

Alternative treatments for depression include talking therapies such as cognitive behavioural therapy (CBT).

Increasingly, people with moderate to severe depression are treated using a combination of antidepressants and CBT. Antidepressants work quickly in reducing symptoms, whereas CBT takes time to deal with causes of depression and ways of overcoming it.

Regular exercise has also been shown to be useful in those with mild depression.

1 October 2013

⇨ The above information is reprinted with kind permission from NHS Choices. Please visit www.nhs.uk for further information.

Pros and cons of medication

Avoid a knee-jerk response either for or against medication. Find out the facts and make an informed decision.

One of many options

Medication (or taking tablets) is simply one of the many options available to help combat depression. It has both benefits and drawbacks. Some people have strong feelings about medication, but it is better to evaluate the pros and cons in a balanced way.

Some of the myths and concerns about taking medication include:

'What's the point of getting "false happiness" which will disappear when I stop taking the pills?'

Antidepressants do not make you 'happy' as such – they help to adjust abnormally low levels of brain chemicals to lift mood to more normal levels. They are most effective when part of a multi-faceted strategy for reversing the depression habit spiral by providing motivation to tackle other unhelpful habits, like depressed thinking, reduced activity levels or disturbed sleep patterns. When continued for six months after remission from depression, antidepressants have been shown to significantly reduce the chance of relapse.

'Pills are a crutch and taking them means I am weak'

So if you break your leg it would be 'weak' to have it in plaster for a while to help it repair, rather than leaving it to mend on its own? Basing a decision about medication on harsh, self-judgemental standards like this is a sign of depressed thinking.

'I don't want to feel like I "need" pills to make me happy'

Again, this is unnecessarily perfectionist. Would you make the same judgement about using contact lenses to see better? The brain's mood chemicals are just another part of our bodies which may not always operate optimally, but which can be corrected with medication (which is usually used temporarily, unlike glasses!).

'So, if I just take some pills it will make it all go away...?'

Actually, NHS guidelines suggest that antidepressants should not be offered in the first instance for mild depression as other strategies may be more effective with fewer side effects. Medication can reverse some of the effects of depression, such as low mood and lack of motivation, and can provide the energy for re-engagement with life, socialising, etc., which helps combat other depressive effects. Medication is most useful when forming part of a combined strategy to tackle the various effects of the depression habit spiral.

'What about these side effects then?'

Newer antidepressants do have fewer side effects, but none of them are side effect free and some side effects, though rare, can be quite serious. Some side effects can be useful, e.g. aiding sleep. The side effects tend to be worst in the first couple of weeks and then many taper off. Make sure you discuss the potential side effects with your doctor, as each type of medication has a slightly different side effect profile. You may need to try a few different types of antidepressant before you find one that suits you.

'I don't want to become addicted'

Antidepressant medication is not addictive. It does not cause craving, and you don't need to take more and more in order to get the same effect. However, it is important that when you stop taking the medication you do so gradually to prevent the unpleasant symptoms of sudden withdrawal.

'I suppose I could get some and just take them when I'm feeling particularly low...'

No, they don't work that way. The medication usually takes several weeks to build up enough in your system to have a beneficial effect (though you may feel some of the side effects straight away). Stopping suddenly or missing doses can cause unpleasant symptoms such as dizziness, nausea, pins and needles, anxiety and headaches.

> **'In both my episodes of depression, medication played an important role for me as it lifted my mood, energy and motivation enough to engage in therapy which I may not have been able to do alone'**
>
> *Iona, 24, north of England*

'I've heard some antidepressants can make you feel suicidal'

Research has shown an increased risk of suicidal thinking on first starting on some antidepressants for people under the age of 18, but no evidence of an increased risk above that age. However, because people mature at different rates and young adults tend to have a higher background risk of suicide, doctors are advised to carefully monitor young adults taking antidepressant medication. This means you should be asked to book a follow-up appointment when you first get prescribed antidepressants. It is very important to attend this and keep in touch with your doctor.

'Although the side effects of the antidepressants resulted in a prolonged suicidal period, the long-term effects were for the best, enabling me to go about life more easily'

It is also important to be aware, if you have been having suicidal thoughts, that when you first take antidepressants your energy and motivation improve before your mood – you can remain suicidal but now have the energy to do it. It is important to look out for increased negativity and hopelessness or sudden changes in mood, as well as suicidal thoughts, and to have regular check-ups with your doctor and good support systems in place. Only you can decide whether this initial risk is worth the potential longer-term benefits.

'Is it worth it? They don't seem to have made much difference for some people I know who've taken them...'

The most recent NHS guidance cites research showing antidepressants are indeed not as beneficial for mild depression as for moderate and severe depression, so should not be prescribed initially in this case. If antidepressants are indicated, it may be necessary to try several varieties before finding the most appropriate pill and dose. Once these factors are taken into account, research shows that 80% of people taking antidepressants experience benefits*.

⇨ The above material is from studentsagainstdepression.org, a project of the Charlie Waller Memorial Trust. Intellectual property rights for the site are owned by Dr Denise Meyer. We are grateful to the Trust for allowing us to use their material.

© Students Against Depression

Treatment options

The kind of treatment that your doctor recommends will be based on the type of depression you have.

Mild depression

Wait and see

If you're diagnosed with mild depression, your depression may improve by itself. In this case, you'll simply be seen again by your GP after two weeks to monitor your progress. This is known as watchful waiting.

Exercise

Exercise has been proven to help depression, and is one of the main treatments if you have mild depression. Your GP may refer you to a qualified fitness trainer for an exercise scheme.

Self-help groups

Talking through your feelings can be helpful. It can be either to a friend or relative, or you can ask your GP to suggest a local self-help group. Your GP may also recommend self-help books and online cognitive behavioural therapy (CBT).

Mild to moderate depression

Talking therapy

If you have mild depression that isn't improving, or you have moderate depression, your GP may recommend a talking treatment (a type of psychotherapy). There are different types of talking therapy for depression including CBT and counselling. Your GP can refer you for talking treatment or, in some parts of the country, you might be able to refer yourself.

Moderate to severe depression

Antidepressants

Antidepressants are tablets that treat the symptoms of depression. There are almost 30 different kinds of antidepressant. They have to be prescribed by a doctor, usually for depression that is moderate or severe.

Combination therapy

Your GP may recommend that you take a course of antidepressants plus talking therapy, particularly if your depression is quite severe. A combination of an antidepressant and CBT usually works better than having just one of these treatments.

Mental health teams

If you have severe depression, you may be referred to a mental health team made up of psychologists, psychiatrists, specialist nurses and occupational therapists. These teams often provide intensive specialist talking treatments as well as prescribed medication.

⇨ The above information is reprinted with kind permission from NHS Choices. Please visit www.nhs.co.uk for further information.

© NHS 2012

Depression over-diagnosed and over-treated

A University of Liverpool study has found that people are increasingly diagnosed and treated with medication for depression when they are suffering 'normal' human experiences such as grief and sadness.

A report published in the *British Medical Journal* (*BMJ*) found that although the prevalence of depressive disorders is stable in the UK and US, rates of diagnosis have increased considerably. In England, antidepressant prescriptions increased by ten per cent a year between 1998 and 2010 and in the US, 11 per cent of over-11s were prescribed antidepressant drugs.

The report identifies a number of factors which are responsible for the increase, including the lowering of the threshold of what constitutes depression. The formal definition of depression was introduced by the *Diagnostic and Statistical Manual of Mental Disorders* (*DSM*) in 1980 and resulted in sadness and grief being diagnosed as depression.

In the most recent version of the manual, *DSM-5* published last year, the definitions of depression have been broadened even further. It now puts a timescale of two weeks for a person to recover from a bereavement after which a depression disorder can be diagnosed.

Professor Chris Dowrick, from the Institute of Psychology, Health and Society who also works as a GP, said: 'Over-diagnosis is now more common than under-diagnosis. Evidence shows that antidepressant medication has little or no effect on mild depression and the passing of time and other means of support generally make people feel better.

'In order to prevent unnecessary medication with its associated side effects, risks and costs, the diagnostic criteria for defining depression need to be tightened up. Instead of prescribing medication, more attention needs to be given to support, advice, social networks and psychological interventions. GPs could then focus on those with serious mental health needs.'

The report also argues that over-diagnosis and over-treatment are the result of heavy drug company marketing, a focus among many psychiatrists on the biology of psychiatric symptoms rather than their psychological, social and cultural aspects, alongside increased requests from patients for medication and subsequent response from GPs.

8 January 2014

⇨ The above information is reprinted with kind permission from The University of Liverpool. Please visit www.news.liv.ac.uk for further information.

Depression: alternatives to drug treatment

Talking therapies, diet, exercise and health supplements – Lesley Dobson examines the alternatives to drug treatment for depression.

If you suspect you could be depressed, talk to your GP. Prompt diagnosis and treatment can stop it becoming worse.

If you have mild depression, and your GP thinks that you're likely to get better without treatment, they may ask to come back in a couple of weeks' time, to see how you're feeling. It's worth asking for advice if there's anything that's causing particular problems – indigestion, for instance, or insomnia. You won't normally be prescribed antidepressants if you have mild depression, although may be given them if you've had more serious depression in the past or if you've been depressed for a long time.

Talking therapies

There are a variety of talking therapies available, but you may have to wait some time for them. The average wait, according to the charity SANE, is around 18 months. The Government is investing millions of pounds in psychological therapies, and aims to eventually cut waiting time to two weeks, but in the meantime, you should ask your GP about the local situation. Some GPs' surgeries have counsellors attached to their practices, which may mean a shorter wait for treatment.

If you can pay for private treatment, your GP may be able to put you in touch with a private therapist. Be sure though, that you choose one who is registered or accredited.

Different approaches

⇨ Cognitive Behavioural Therapy (CBT): focuses on teaching you to challenge negative thought patterns.

⇨ Psychodynamic Therapy: helps you to look at difficulties in your past and deal with feelings of guilt, aggression and inadequacy.

⇨ Counselling: allows you to talk about your life, and the areas that may be influencing your feelings of depression.

⇨ Interpersonal Therapy (IPT): looks at your relationships with others and helps you improve how you see yourself.

Talking therapies and antidepressants may work better if you have both at the same time.

Exercise

Taking a brisk walk may sound old-fashioned, but studies have shown that regular exercise can help you feel better, and sometimes prevent depression developing in the first place.

Exercise triggers the release of your body's feel-good chemicals, endorphins, which may help ease your symptoms. Taking exercise also gives you targets to aim for, and gets you up and out and meeting people.

30 minutes' moderate exercise, five or more days a week, should be the minimum that we all aim for. You can do this on your own, with a friend, or join a club. Your GP may also be able to refer you for 'Exercise on Prescription'. There are around 1,300 of these schemes in the UK. Ask your GP if there's one near you.

Diet

A balanced diet, with at least five portions of fruit and vegetables every day, plenty of fibre, some protein and small amounts of fat and salt, should help keep your health on track. But if you don't feel physically well, you're less likely to feel emotionally well and positive. And if you're lacking certain nutrients it can have an impact on your mental health. Protein, for instance, contains the amino acid tryptophan, which affects your mood.

Low levels of omega-3 oils – found in oily fish such as mackerel, sardines and salmon, flaxseed oil, rapeseed oil and walnuts – are also linked to depression. A number of small studies have shown that giving omega-3 oils alongside conventional drug treatment improved patients' symptoms.

It's also important to watch what you drink. Keeping your non-alcoholic fluids up is important, as dehydration can affect you mentally, making you confused and irritable. Keeping to a moderate alcohol intake is also important as alcohol is a depressant.

St John's Wort

St John's Wort is a herbal remedy that is known to help ease the symptoms of mild to moderate depression. It's available over the counter, but GPs aren't allowed to prescribe it. While it can be helpful, take it with caution, as it can react with other medicines. If you are on other medication, talk to your GP or pharmacist before taking St John's Wort. You shouldn't take it if you're already taking SSRI or MAOI antidepressants.

St John's Wort is widely available, but it can come in varying strengths and preparations depending on the brand, so read the label carefully. It can take up to four weeks to have any effect.

*The opinions expressed are those of the author and are not held by Saga unless specifically stated.

The material is for general information only and does not constitute investment, tax, legal, medical or other form of advice. You should not rely on this information to make (or refrain from making) any decisions. Always obtain independent, professional advice for your own particular situation.

⇨ The above information is reprinted with kind permission from Saga Magazine. Please visit www.saga.co.uk/magazine for further information.

The NHS is 'failing to treat depressed patients'

In 2012/13, GPs made 883,963 referrals for psychological support in England...

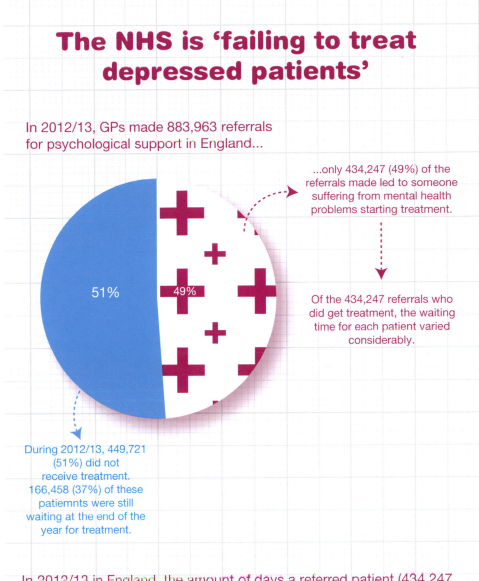

...only 434,247 (49%) of the referrals made led to someone suffering from mental health problems starting treatment.

Of the 434,247 referrals who did get treatment, the waiting time for each patient varied considerably.

During 2012/13, 449,721 (51%) did not receive treatment. 166,458 (37%) of these patiemnts were still waiting at the end of the year for treatment.

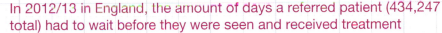

In 2012/13 in England, the amount of days a referred patient (434,247 total) had to wait before they were seen and received treatment

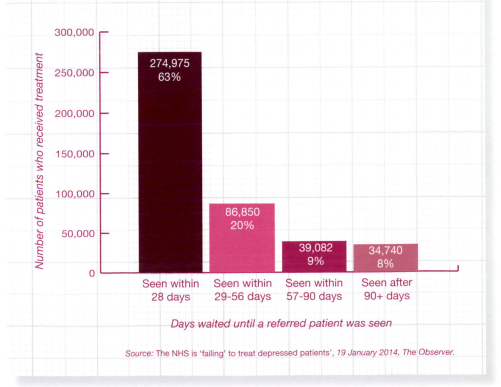

Days waited until a referred patient was seen

Source: The NHS is 'failing' to treat depressed patients', 19 January 2014, The Observer.

Talking therapy

Talking therapy can help you deal with psychological factors involved in your depression.

There are lots of different types of talking therapy to suit all situations and people.

Choosing a therapy

Before you make your choice, think about:

What treatment would suit me? For example, do you think you'd prefer to deal with the here-and-now, or would you rather look at the past?

⇨ How long will I have to wait?

⇨ How long will the therapy last?

⇨ Does it cost anything?

⇨ Have I any preference about who I see – a man or woman, older or younger?

⇨ Who may be able to recommend a therapist to me?

Which therapies work?

Researchers have found the following treatments to be effective in treating depression.

⇨ Behavioural activation helps you get back into activities that you have stopped.

⇨ Cognitive Behavioural Therapy (CBT) is based on the here and now. It focuses on what we do (Behaviour) and how it influences the way we think (Cognitive) and vice versa to help make changes.

⇨ Couple-focused therapy can help if your relationship is contributing to your depression. The therapist will work to change the way you and your partner interact so you develop a more supportive relationship.

⇨ Interpersonal Therapy (IPT) helps you find new ways to get along with others and looks at problems in your relationships.

⇨ Mindfulness Based Cognitive Therapy (MBCT) is based on the importance of being aware of the present moment and not worrying over the past or future.

⇨ Problem-solving therapy helps you find out what your problems are, work out what your aims are and come up with ways of achieving them.

⇨ Psychodynamic psychotherapy looks at how past experiences affect people. It also looks at the relationship between the therapist and the client and how that is affected by the past.

⇨ Counselling offers a safe space for you to explore your feelings. Counselling is commonly offered as a talking therapy for depression.

Other talking therapies don't have so much evidence. This doesn't mean they don't work, just that more research may be needed.

⇨ Cognitive analytic therapy which uses parts of Cognitive Behavioural Therapy and psychodynamic therapy.

⇨ Eye movement desensitisation and reprocessing (EMDR) helps with trauma.

⇨ Family therapy deals with problems in the family.

⇨ Hypnotherapy uses hypnosis to change how we feel.

⇨ Neurolinguistic programming (NLP) is used to detect and change unconscious thoughts and behaviours.

⇨ Reminiscence therapy involves looking at how the past affects the present.

⇨ Transactional analysis (TA) looks at how we relate to other people.

Finally, if you are a more practical person you may want to try:

⇨ Art therapy where you express your feelings and emotions through art.

⇨ Music therapy where you use music to express how you feel.

⇨ The above information is reprinted with kind permission from Action on Depression, Scotland's national charity for depression. Please visit www.actionondepression.org for further information.

© Action on Depression 2014

Depression and cognitive behavioural therapy

Research shows cognitive behavioural therapy is effective for depressed patients.

By Siski Green

For some patients, antidepressants give near-immediate relief from the symptoms of depression, which may include fatigue, feelings of hopelessness or worthlessness and loss of interest in activities or hobbies, for example. But for many, the same medications just don't work. They may alleviate the symptoms to some extent but not fully, they may not work at all, or the side effects may be too great to make the medication helpful.

New research shows that cognitive behavioural therapy, when used along with usual care, can be as effective in patients who don't respond to medication.

Cognitive behavioural therapy (CBT) involves a therapist talking through a patient's current thoughts and feelings (rather than focusing on the past, as some other forms of therapy do) and then suggesting ways in which a person can change those habitual thought patterns and beliefs. Different coping strategies are suggested and a person's overall approach to life, their way of viewing themselves and others, can be altered so that mental well-being is improved. Researchers from the Universities of Bristol, Exeter and Glasgow recruited 469 patients in order to assess how effective CBT was in helping to relieve symptoms of depression in those for whom medications did not work. All the patients were classified as having treatment-resistant depression.

They were split into two groups – one group continued to get the usual care from their GP, including continuing to take medication; the other group also got the usual care, including medication, but they also had cognitive behavioural therapy.

The participants were checked at six months and then a year afterwards to see how effective the therapy had been. At the six-month point nearly half of the CBT group had improved, compared to just 22% of the other non-CBT group. Improvement was classed as when a participant showed at least a 50% reduction in symptoms of depression. This benefit was maintained over the year.

These are important findings, say the researchers, as they suggest that although antidepressants are most often the first treatment offered to patients, CBT should be offered more routinely to patients worldwide.

In the UK, CBT is available on the NHS to depressed patients who haven't shown improvements with other forms of treatment.

It is possible to use CBT methods in other ways – self-help books with exercises can be useful, and you can also utilise a computer-based CBT program. Some are free and there are many others that require payment. Ask your GP to recommend one that would work best for you.

*The opinions expressed are those of the author and are not held by Saga unless specifically stated.

The material is for general information only and does not constitute investment, tax, legal, medical or other form of advice. You should not rely on this information to make (or refrain from making) any decisions. Always obtain independent, professional advice for your own particular situation.

14 December 2012

⇨ The above information is reprinted with kind permission from Saga Magazine. Please visit www.saga.co.uk/magazine for further information.

Males think that talking about problems is a waste of time

Males have difficulty discussing their problems with others because they tend to not think it is particularly useful – according to a new study.

By William Smith

Dr Amanda J. Rose, associate professor of psychological sciences at the University of Missouri and researcher for this study says: 'For some years, popular psychologists have insisted that boys and men would like to talk about their problems but are held back by fears of embarrassment or appearing weak.'

'However, when we asked young people how talking about their problems would make them feel, boys didn't express angst or distress about discussing problems any more than girls. Instead, boys' responses suggest that they just don't see talking about problems to be a particularly useful activity.'

Four different studies were conducted by researchers that include surveys and observations of nearly 2,000 children and adolescents. They found that girls had positive expectations for how talking about problems would make them feel. These expectations included feeling card for, understood and less alone.

Boys, surprisingly, were no more likely than girls to say that talking about problems would cause them to be embarrassed or worried that they would be teased. Instead, boys reported that talking about problems would make them feel 'weird, and like they were 'wasting time.'

Rose said: 'An implication is that parents should encourage their children to adopt a middle ground when discussing problems. For boys, it would be helpful to explain that, at least or some problems, some of the time, talking about their problems is not a waste of time. Yet parents also should realise that they may be "barking up the wrong tree" if they think that making boys feel safer will make them confide. Instead, helping boys see some utility in talking about problems may be more effective.'

The findings may play into future romantic relationships, as many relationships involve a 'pursuit-withdraw cycle' in which one partner (usually the woman) pursues talking about problems while the other (usually the man) withdraws, Rose believes.

The paper will be published in a future edition of the journal *Child Development*.

Source: University of Missouri

⇨ The above information is reprinted with kind permission from Mental Healthy. Please visit www. mentalhealthy.co.uk for further information.

Depression symptoms may be improved by acupuncture or counselling

Acupuncture or counselling, provided alongside usual care, could benefit patients with depression, a recent study has revealed.

The study, conducted by researchers at the University of York, found the combination of acupuncture or counselling with usual care had some benefits after three months for patients with recurring depression.

While the news may be welcomed by patients keen to receive non-drug therapies, scientists were quick to point out there is limited evidence to support the use of acupuncture or counselling for depression.

Lead author Dr Hugh MacPherson says in a statement: 'Although these findings are encouraging, our study does not identify which aspects of acupuncture and counselling are likely to be most beneficial to patients, nor does it provide information about the effectiveness of acupuncture or counselling, compared with usual care, for patients with mild depression.'

The research team randomised patients with depression to receive 12 weekly sessions of acupuncture plus usual care (302 patients), or 12 weekly sessions of counselling plus usual care (302 patients) or usual care alone (151 patients).

The groups that received acupuncture and counselling showed a significant reduction in average depression scores at three months, compared with usual care alone.

But, there was no significant difference in depression scores between the acupuncture and counselling groups. At nine months and 12 months, because of improvements in the depression scores in the usual care group,

acupuncture and counselling were no longer better than usual care.

Dr MacPherson added: 'To our knowledge, our study is the first to rigorously evaluate the clinical and economic impact of acupuncture and counselling for patients in primary care who are representative of those who continue to experience depression in primary care.'

He adds: 'We have provided evidence that acupuncture versus usual care and counselling versus usual care are both associated with a significant reduction in symptoms of depression in the short to medium term, and are not associated with serious adverse events.'

The study was published this week in *PLOS Medicine* and also involved researchers from the Centre for Health Economics at York and Hull York Medical School. It was funded by the National Institute for Health Research (NIHR) Programme Grants for Applied Research Programme.

25 September 2013

⇨ The above information is reprinted with kind permission from *Huffington Post UK*. Please visit www.huffingtonpost.co.uk for further information.

Surfing on prescription helps kids at breaking point

The NHS is funding a pilot programme that prescribes surfing lessons for young people with depression and low self-esteem. Based in Dorset, the Wave Project is open to people aged between eight and 21 who have been referred by mental health services, schools or social services.

By Jess Ponting, Director of the Centre for Surf Research at San Diego State University

The idea of using surfing for complementary mental health benefits and empowering young people isn't new. All over the world, programmes have been established to introduce at-risk and low-income youth to surfing to positively impact their lives. Along these lines, the Dorset project, run by volunteers, aims to build up the confidence, self-esteem, motivation and emotional resilience of its young participants. For many people the idea might provoke a chuckle, but how legitimate is the claim that surfing and a connection with the ocean might change your life?

'Stoke'

The data from the project, 100 questionnaires filled in by young people before and after the surfing course, falls short of demonstrating that surfing itself makes a positive difference – as opposed to a more generic effect from skills and team building. But it would be remiss to overlook the power of what surfers refer to as 'stoke': a force that has been driving humans back to the ocean for physical rejuvenation and spiritual balance for thousands of years.

The first European account of surfing was by William Anderson, surgeon to Captain James Cook, who noted the actions of a Tahitian fisherman in an outrigger canoe in Matavai Bay in 1777. Anderson watched the fisherman paddling frantically to catch a wave before riding it to shore and then, against all logic, turn around and paddle back out to ride another. And another. Anderson wrote:

He went out from the shore till he was near the place where the swell begins to take its rise; and, watching its first motion very attentively, paddled before it with great quickness, till he found that it overlooked him, and had acquired sufficient force to carry his canoe before it without passing underneath. He then sat motionless, and was carried along at the same swift rate as the wave, till it landed him upon the beach.

Anderson said he 'could not help concluding that this man felt the most supreme pleasure while he was driven on so fast and so smoothly by the sea'. Stoke. It has driven all kinds of people to the sea from pre-Incan Chan Chan fishermen, in what is now Peru, surfing little reed fishing boats, to coastal settlements across Polynesia and Melanesia including Hawaii where surfing reached its peak cultural expression.

Stoke appears to transcend culture, time and space. From a historic low of perhaps several thousand surfers at the turn of the 20th century, there are now 77 member countries of the International Surfing Association

Get the lingo

Rad

Really awesome or cool; crazy, insane, weird, unplanned.

Goofy foot

Surfing with the left foot on the back of board (right foot is regular).

Wipe-out

Falling or being knocked off your surfboard when riding a wave.

Squid

A beginner or newcomer.

Floater

Riding up on the top of the breaking part of the wave and coming down with it.

Over the falls or the wash cycle

Falling off your board and the wave sucks you up in a circular motion along with the wave's lip.

and some estimates suggest that there are as many as 35 million surfers worldwide accessing surf in 161 countries. There are few, if any, other activities that demand such a deep and enduring commitment from its participants, and a very literal immersion in the natural environment and the forces of nature.

'It would be remiss to overlook the power of what surfers refer to as "stoke": a force that has been driving humans back to the ocean for physical rejuvenation and spiritual balance for thousands of years'

Breaking waves

New York science prodigy Venzen Wu, who identified a new antibiotic from carnivorous pitcher plants at age ten, learned to surf in California on a break from Colombia University. He was immediately hooked and intrigued by the feelings of elation that accompanied surfing. He linked stoke to negative ions – atoms with more than the usual number of electrons – which have been shown to increase serotonin levels and improve mood in clinical testing. Negative ions are created in nature where air and water collide – like around breaking waves.

In an interview with world-renowned surf journalist Tim Baker, Wu hypothesised that if negative ions are responsible for stoke, there are 'significant implications for the treatment of depression and other mental disorder … the treatment of depression could become as easy as a day at the beach'.

In my own research with Canadian-based sociologist Alan Law, we've begun to look at the value of stoke and community that surfing can provide for people who may be on the fringes of 'normal' society. Those who are emotionally fragile or depressed who could access feelings of community and worth beyond normal social measures like wealth and title. We make the case that stoke not only benefits surfers, but the communities in which they live as well. At the San Diego State University Center for Surf Research we are now leveraging stoke to open students from around the world up to sustainability education in study abroad classes to world-class surfing destinations.

Whatever is causing it, the surfing community is driven by stoke and will tell you that it is one of the more powerful forces in their lives. Surfers would be way more surprised if surfing didn't help people with depression, build confidence, self-esteem and motivation, and prescription surf lessons are a great way to reach out to people in need.

28 November 2013

⇨ The above information is reprinted with kind permission from The Conversation. Please visit www.theconversation.com for further information.

Self-help books aid depression

A new study has suggested self-help books should be prescribed by the health service as they could benefit people with depression.

By Jess Laurence

The study's leader, Professor Christopher Williams from Glasgow University, said depressed people who were given self-help literature along with sessions advising them how to use the books, had 'lower levels' of depression after a year.

Over 200 depressed patients participated in the study. Around 50% of the group were taking antidepressant medication prescribed by their GPs.

After a four-month period, the patients who read self-help books and had three sessions with an adviser had 'significantly lower' levels of depression compared to patients who only saw their GPs.

Professor Williams commented: 'We found this had a really significant clinical impact and the findings are very encouraging.'

'Depression saps people's motivation and makes it hard to believe change is possible.'

Dr Paul Blenkiron, consultant in adult psychiatry at Leeds and York Partnership NHS Foundation Trust, said the research revealed that self-help alongside guided sessions worked and was 'something the NHS should be investing in'.

21 January 2013

⇨ The above information is reprinted with kind permission from Healthcare Today. Please visit www.healthcare-today.co.uk for further information.

UK study into whether physical activity aids depression finds no additional benefit

*Current clinical guidance recommends physical activity to alleviate the symptoms of depression. However, new research published in the **BMJ**, suggests that adding a physical activity intervention to usual care did not reduce symptoms of depression more than usual care alone, even though it increased levels of physical activity.*

Depression is one of the most common reasons for seeking GP help and reportedly affects one in six adults in Britain at any one time. Until now, most of the evidence for the positive effect of physical activity in treating depression has originated from studies of small, non-clinical samples using interventions that would not be practicable in an NHS setting.

The TREAD study, led by researchers from the Universities of Bristol, Exeter and the Peninsula College of Medicine and Dentistry, is the first large-scale, randomised controlled trial to establish whether a physical activity intervention should be used in primary health care to help treat adults with depression.

Researchers recruited 361 patients aged 18–69 years who had recently been diagnosed with depression. Trial participants were then split into two groups to receive either the physical activity intervention in addition to usual care or usual care on its own and were followed up for 12 months to assess any change in their symptoms.

Melanie Chalder, from University of Bristol's School of Social and Community Medicine, said: 'Numerous studies have reported the positive effects of physical activity for people suffering with depression but our intervention was not an effective strategy for reducing symptoms. However, it is important to note that increased physical activity is beneficial for people with other medical conditions such as obesity, diabetes and cardiovascular disease and, of course, these conditions can affect people with depression.'

John Campbell, Professor of General Practice and Primary Care at Peninsula College of Medicine and Dentistry (University of Exeter), commented: 'Many patients suffering from depression would prefer not to have to take traditional antidepressant medication, preferring instead to consider alternative non-drug-based forms of therapy. Exercise and activity appeared to offer promise as one such treatment, but this carefully designed research study has shown that exercise does not appear to be effective in treating depression. An important finding, however, is the observation that the approach we were using did result in a sustained increase in activity in people who were working with our activity facilitators. Although their increased activity did not result in improved depression, the approach we used offers potential in areas other than depression, and we hope to explore this in due course.'

Adrian Taylor, Professor of Sport and Health Sciences at the University of Exeter, added: 'We were pleased that people responded to the tailored physical activity intervention, which focused on increasing sustainable moderate intensity physical activity. However, reducing depression more than is possible through usual care is clearly a huge challenge.'

The study was funded as part of the National Institute for Health Research (NIHR) Health Technology Assessment (HTA) programme, with contributions from the Department of Health and local primary care trusts. The paper entitled 'Facilitated physical activity as a treatment for depressed adults: randomised controlled trial', is published in the BMJ (*British Medical Journal*) and will be presented as a keynote paper at the World Family Doctors Caring for People (WONCA) conference in Vienna in July 2012.

6 June 2012

⇨ The above information is reprinted with kind permission from the University of Exeter. Please visit www.sshs.exeter.ac.uk for further information.

© *University of Exeter 2012*

Why the object of exercise is not just a physical one: regular exercise lowers depression risk by up to 30 per cent

By Jonathan Owen

Just ten minutes' brisk walking can improve your emotional state, according to a report being released by the Mental Health Foundation to mark the start of Mental Health Awareness Week.

Taking part in regular physical activity can both increase self-esteem and reduce stress and anxiety, according to the report.

And it can act as both prevention and treatment for various mental illnesses including depression and anxiety.

'One way to enhance our mental well-being and protect our mental health is through participating in physical activity,' it states.

And people who exercise regularly have a 20–30 per cent lower risk for depression and dementia.

The report suggests using physical activity to 'regulate mood during the day' but warns against overdoing it – for this could result in 'short-lived negative effects' such as 'low mood and irritability'. 'People should choose a type of physical activity based on what they enjoy doing,' it adds.

But it warns that most people are not doing anywhere near enough exercise, with just 40 per cent of men and 28 per cent of women in the UK managing the two-and-a-half hours a week recommended by the NHS.

12 May 2013

⇨ The above information is reprinted with kind permission from *The Independent*. Please visit www.independent.co.uk for further information.

Exercise for depression

It has long been known that regular exercise is good for our physical health. It can reduce the risk of cancer, heart disease and strokes.

In recent years, studies have shown that regular physical activity also has benefits for mental health. Exercise can help people with depression and prevent them from becoming depressed in the first place.

Dr Alan Cohen, a GP with a special interest in mental health, says that when people get depressed or anxious, they often feel they're not in control of their lives.

'Exercise gives them back control of their bodies and this is often the first step to feeling in control of other events,' he says.

Who can benefit and what type of exercise is best?

Anyone with depression can benefit from doing regular exercise, but it's especially useful for people with mild depression.

'Any type of exercise is useful as long as it suits you and you do enough of it,' says Dr Cohen. 'Exercise should be something you enjoy. Otherwise it will be hard to find the motivation to do it regularly.'

How often do you need to exercise?

To stay healthy, adults should do 150 minutes of moderate-intensity activity every week.

If you haven't exercised for a while, gradually introduce physical activity into your daily routine.

Even a 15-minute walk can help you clear your mind and relax. Any exercise is better than none.

How to get started

Take part in a team sport, attend classes at a sports centre or just be more active in your daily routine by walking or cycling instead of travelling by car.

Find an activity you can do regularly.

To find local exercise classes and sports clubs, search the sport and fitness directory on the NHS website.

If conservation work appeals to you, look at the Green Gym website (www.tcv.org.uk). Green Gym projects, run in association with The Conservation Volunteers (TCV), provide exercise for people who don't like the idea of a sports or leisure centre. A typical project involves working in local woodlands or creating community gardens. Sessions are free and led by a TCV member of staff.

⇨ The above information is reprinted with kind permission from NHS Choices. Please visit www.nhs.uk for further information.

'I run to boost my mood'

Liz Gardiner is a GP in Leicester. She describes her experience of depression and how a combination of medication, therapy and exercise has helped her.

By Liz Gardiner, Leicester GP

'I've had depression since I was a teenager. It was really bad in my early teens but I didn't seek help until I was about 15. My GP was really helpful and supportive.

'Over a couple of years, I tried five or six different types of antidepressant until we finally found one that worked for me and that I still take today. It really seems to sort my brain chemistry out.

'I'm quite happy with the fact that I'm probably going to take antidepressants every day for the rest of my life. I've tried to stop a couple of times but my symptoms come back. If I don't take them, I feel like I can't cope, whereas if I do, I feel normal.

'I had various different talking therapies when I was at medical school in my early twenties, including cognitive behavioural therapy (CBT) and general counselling. I found both very helpful and I still use the positive thinking strategies I learned.

'CBT teaches you to change the way you think and to question your negative thoughts.

'For example, if you've arranged to meet a friend in town and the friend doesn't turn up on time, somebody who's not prone to depression might think it's a pain and then go and get a coffee while waiting to hear from the friend.

'But if you're prone to depression, you might start thinking, "Is it because they don't like me any more?", "Have I done something wrong?" or "How could they do this to me?"'

Coping with depression

If you've been feeling down for more than two weeks, see your GP to discuss your symptoms. They can tell you about the treatments available and what might be best for you.

'One of the strategies I learned through CBT is to identify the thoughts that make me feel bad and to question them. By questioning my negative thoughts, I would realise that it's probably not that my friend doesn't like me any more and more likely that his bus was late.

'It helps you to be more rational. Instead of assuming that you're a terrible person and the world's awful, you look for alternative explanations, which make you feel less negative.

'Having supportive friends has also really helped me. In the past, I wouldn't ask for help from other people if I was feeling low. I would try to deal with it on my own and pretend to everyone else that I was completely OK.

'Over time I've learned that it's really helpful to explain how you're feeling to someone close and get some support. I've realised that it's much easier to talk to other people than to try to cope with your thoughts on your own.

'I'm lucky to have a fantastic group of friends. We met in the first year of medical school and we've helped each other through all the ups and downs of training to be doctors.

'For the past four years, running has been a big part of my life.

'I'm a different person when I exercise regularly. When I run two or three times a week my energy and my motivation lift. I think running really does help protect me from depression. When I don't run regularly I'm more prone to feeling low.

'I used to have a gym subscription but would only go once a month. I always intended to do more exercise but hardly ever got round to it. Then a friend of mine ran the London Marathon and I decided I wanted to do the same thing the following year. I ran the London Marathon in 2006 and every autumn I do the Great North Run in Newcastle.

'To make sure I run regularly, I find that I need to develop a structured exercise programme for myself. On Tuesdays and Thursdays, I take my running stuff with me to work and on the way home I'll stop at the local park and go running. If I go home first, I sit down and then don't feel like going out again. I've tried to build exercise into my routine. That way I don't have to think about doing it. It's part of a normal day.

'I haven't been unwell with depression for five years now. Although I know I could slip back into being depressed, I feel I have several options to help me if my mood starts dipping.

'Doing exercise and keeping my body healthy keeps my spirits up. CBT makes my brain work in a different way. I stop and question myself now instead of falling into a downward spiral. I get lots of support from friends and then there's the underlying treatment with antidepressants.'

⇨ The above information is reprinted with kind permission from NHS Choices. Please visit www.nhs.uk for further information.

THE CONVERSATION

Green cities provide a mental health boost that lasts

An article from The Conversation.

By Ian Alcock, Associate Research Fellow at University of Exeter

It's been established that enjoying green spaces in otherwise grey urban areas can lead to improved mental health for city-dwellers. But new research has revealed how surprisingly quickly those benefits appear, and how long they last.

Research from the University of Exeter's European Centre for Environment and Human Health found that people living in towns and cities with more parks and gardens tend to report greater well-being than those without. But it also revealed that relocating to a greener part of town led to improvements in their mental health that lasted for at least three years.

There are other life changes that influence mental health, and many of those do so gradually, or else seem to be only short-lived. Job promotion and marriage boost well-being in the short term, for example, and financial windfalls can lead to gradual improvements. But these new findings indicate that simply increasing the ratio of green to grey in urban neighbourhoods is likely to provide benefits that are not only immediate, but which continue to deliver benefits long afterwards.

The research, just published in the journal *Environmental Science and Technology*, used data from the British Household Panel Survey, a long-running household survey project, based in Essex. We analysed five consecutive years of mental health questionnaires, answered by people who had relocated to a different residential area between the second and third years.

Two groups of people were tracked: 600 who moved to greener urban areas, and 470 who moved to areas that were less green. While the group who moved to greener suburbs showed significant improvements for all three years after their relocation, there was not a corresponding decline in mental health for those who moved to less green areas. There was, however, a decline in the mental health of these people in the year before they moved. It's not clear whether this was some degree of dread at the anticipated relocation, or whether it was declining well-being that lay behind the decision to relocate.

Studying people who relocate from one area to another can offer insights into the effects of town planning decisions that alter the make-up of city neighbourhoods. It's hard to design and carry out experiments that involve the radical 're-greening' and 'de-greening' of our cities to see what effects these processes have. But we can get important clues by looking at the average effects that result from the loss or gain of green space after someone has moved home.

The benefits we've observed have implications for planning policy, which aims to improve public health through urban design. Our findings suggest that improved mental health is not the result simply of the novelty of living in a greener area, which might wear off quickly. Creating parks and green corridors in our increasingly urban landscapes could represent good value-for-money public health services, delivering long-term benefits to community health.

How good is green space for urban residents? An earlier study published in *Psychological Science* estimated the effects on mental health delivered by a 1% difference in urban green space, also working with Household Panel Survey data from England and controlling for the effects of personality. The study found that living in an area with high rather than low green space was equal to roughly a third of the benefit of being married, and a tenth of the benefit of having a job.

Importantly, in estimating the effects of green space, the team accounted for other factors which can influence mental health, such as the individuals' income, family and employment circumstances. They also accounted for area factors which may overlap with urban greenness, such as the socio-economic profile of the neighbourhood.

Depression and depressive disorders are now the leading cause of disability in middle to high income countries – mental health is a critical public health issue of modern times. And it's quite possible this trend is related to how quickly the world's population is moving to the city: in the world's more developed regions, more than three-quarters of the population live in urban environments, with the reduced access to the natural world that brings.

So while these studies don't show that relocating to a greener area will definitely increase happiness, the findings fit with other experimental work that shows how short spells in a green space does improve people's mood, and cognitive functioning. Our findings join those from earlier epidemiological studies that clearly demonstrate the link between health benefits and green space.

16 January 2014

⇨ The above information is reprinted with kind permission from The Conversation. Please visit www.theconversation.com for further information.

What is SPARX?

SPARX is a computer program that helps young people with mild to moderate depression. It can also help if you're feeling anxious or stressed. It was developed with the help of young people and is based on a type of 'talking therapy' called Cognitive Behavioural Therapy, or CBT for short. You can do CBT with a counsellor or a psychologist but you can also learn CBT skills from a computer program like SPARX. What makes computerised CBT (like SPARX) unique is that you can do it on your own, at your own pace, whenever and wherever it suits you; all you need is a computer with access to the Internet.

CBT focuses on the links between how people think (their 'cognitions'), what they do (their 'behaviour') and how they feel. CBT teaches skills about how to cope with negative thoughts and feelings by helping people to think in a more balanced and helpful way and getting them to do things they enjoy or that give them a sense of achievement. There is lots of research to show that CBT helps.

SPARX can help you learn how to have Smart, Positive, Active, Realistic, X-factor thoughts (SPARX)!

How does SPARX work?

At the start of SPARX you will meet the Guide. The Guide explains what SPARX is and how it could help you. You will then customise your avatar and journey to the seven provinces to complete quests that restore the world's balance and defeat the pesky negative thoughts, called Gnats. Along the way, you will meet different characters, solve puzzles and complete mini games.

As you complete each quest, the Guide will explain how you can use your new skills to feel better, solve problems and enjoy life in the real world.

Each level takes about half an hour. Try doing one or two levels each week.

SPARX is made to help young people who are feeling down, depressed or anxious. If you want to see if SPARX is right for you, take our mood quiz.

Research

We tested SPARX in a large study in New Zealand and the results were published in the *British Medical Journal* in 2012. In addition, three doctoral projects evaluated SPARX with specific groups of young people.

Between 2009 and 2010 we conducted an evaluation (a randomised controlled trial) of SPARX with 187 young people to see if it was effective in treating the symptoms of depression. We compared SPARX with standard care provided to young people with mild to moderate depression, e.g. face-to-face therapy with a counsellor or clinical psychologist.

In our study, 94 young people received SPARX and 93 young people received standard care.

We interviewed young people and asked them to fill in questionnaires to measure depression, anxiety and their quality of life. Information was collected before and after SPARX (or standard care) and three months later.

We found that:

⇨ SPARX was as effective as standard care for adolescents 12- to 19-years-old seeking help for depression;

⇨ SPARX reduced depression, anxiety, feelings of hopelessness and improved quality of life;

⇨ These changes lasted for at least three months;

⇨ SPARX worked better for those with more depression (but still within mild-moderate range);

⇨ SPARX worked equally well across different ethnic groups in New Zealand;

⇨ SPARX worked equally well for girls and boys and older and younger adolescents;

⇨ SPARX appeared to work better when users completed at least half of the modules (i.e. at least four levels);

⇨ Most young people completed at least half of SPARX and this compared very well with other similar programs; and

⇨ Most participants found SPARX useful, believed it would appeal to other teenagers and would recommend it to their friends.

SPARX among young people who are not in mainstream education

This research was carried out by Dr Terry Fleming.

Dr Fleming investigated whether SPARX is acceptable and effective for adolescents who are in alternative education programmes. Young people in alternative education programmes have high rates of depression and other health difficulties and yet have more difficulty accessing health services than students in ordinary schools do.

Dr Fleming's studies showed that:

⇨ SPARX is effective and acceptable for young people attending alternative education; and

⇨ Young people attending alternative education reported that SPARX helped them to deal with anger, reduced their fighting and made them calmer.

Check out these publications for more detail.

Fleming, T., R. Dixon, et al. (2012). ''It's mean!' the views of young people alienated from mainstream education on depression, help seeking and computerised therapy.' Advances in Mental Health 10(2): 196–204

Fleming, T. and S. Merry (2012). 'Youth Work Service Providers' Attitudes Towards Computerized CBT for Adolescents.' Behavioural and Cognitive Psychotherapy FirstView: 1-15.

Fleming, T., R. Dixon, et al. (2012). 'A Pragmatic Randomized Controlled Trial of Computerized CBT (SPARX) for Symptoms of Depression among Adolescents Excluded from Mainstream Education.' Behavioural and Cognitive Psychotherapy 40(05): 529-541.

'Rainbow SPARX' for same/both-sex attracted youth

This research was led by Dr Mathijs Lucassen.

Dr Lucassen developed and evaluated a custom-made version of SPARX called 'Rainbow SPARX' for young people attracted to the same sex or both sexes and those not sure of their sexual attractions (same/both-sex attracted youth). Same/both-sex attracted youth are more likely to experience depression and to have difficulty accessing healthcare for an emotional problem.

Dr Lucassen's research showed that:

⇨ Rainbow SPARX was effective in reducing symptoms of depression and anxiety for same/both-sex attracted youth;

⇨ Rainbow SPARX was an acceptable program for same/both-sex attracted youth; and

⇨ Users found SPARX helpful in overcoming the barriers of geographical and social isolation.

Information for parents

SPARX is a computerised self-help program designed for 12–19-year-olds. It was tested with 187 adolescents from around New Zealand. Our research found that SPARX helped teenagers who were feeling down, depressed or anxious. Most young people who started the program finished it and in general most found SPARX to be very helpful.

If you think your child needs further assistance with their mental health please make an appointment for them to see their GP. You may also want to speak to people at Lifeline or Youthline. They're able to listen to you and will help you find ways of helping your child. Living with someone with depression or anxiety can be difficult, and they can help you find ways to make this easier for you.

Awards for SPARX

UN and Netexplo awards for SPARX

SPARX won an international digital award from Netexplo, a 'global observatory on digital society', hosted by UNESCO. The awards were presented for projects that Netexplo call 'the ten most innovative and promising digital initiatives of the year'.

SPARX also won a 2011 World Summit Award in the category of e-Health and Environment. The World Summit Awards honour excellence in multimedia and e-Content creation. 40 winners (five in each category) are selected from 100 countries. The World Summit Awards are under the auspices of United Nations.

⇨ The above information is reprinted with kind permission from SPARX. Please visit www.sparx.org.nz and http://linkedwellness.com/ for further information. Please note that SPARX is not currently publically available in the UK.

Great dream

Ten keys to happier living.

Action for Happiness has developed the 'Ten Keys to Happier Living' based on a review of the latest scientific research relating to happiness.

Everyone's path to happiness is different, but the research suggests these ten things consistently tend to have a positive impact on people's overall happiness and well-being.

The first five relate to how we interact with the **outside** world in our daily activities. The second five come more from **inside** us and depend on our attitude to life.

GIVING Do things for others

RELATING Connect with people

EXERCISING Take care of your body

APPRECIATING Notice the world around

TRYING OUT Keep learning new things

DIRECTION Have goals to look forward to

RESILIENCE Find ways to bounce back

EMOTION Take a positive approach

ACCEPTANCE Be comfortable with who you are

MEANING Be part of something bigger

What do the ten keys mean for you?

The ten keys are explained in more detail below. Each key has a related question to help us think about how it applies in our own lives. There are no right or wrong answers – it's just helpful to reflect on these different aspects of our lives.

GIVING: do things for others

Helping others is not only good for them and a good thing to do, it also makes us happier and healthier too. Giving also connects us to others, creating stronger communities and helping to build a happier society for everyone. And it's not all about money – we can also give our time, ideas and energy. So if you want to feel good, do good!

Q: What do you do to help others?

'Learning to accept ourselves, warts and all, and being kinder to ourselves when things go wrong, increases our enjoyment of life, our resilience and our well-being. It also helps us accept others as they are'

RELATING: connect with people

People with strong and broad social relationships are happier, healthier and live longer. Close relationships with family and friends provide love, meaning, support and increase our feelings of self-worth. Broader networks bring a sense of belonging. So taking action to strengthen our relationships and build connections is essential for happiness.

Q: Who matters most to you?

EXERCISING: take care of your body

Our body and our mind are connected. Being active makes us happier as well as being good for our physical health. It instantly improves our mood and can even lift us out of a depression. We don't all need to run marathons – there are simple things we can all do to be more active each day. We can also boost our well-being by unplugging from technology, getting outside and making sure we get enough sleep!

Q: How do you stay active and healthy?

APPRECIATING: notice the world around

Ever felt there must be more to life? Well good news,

there is! And it's right here in front of us. We just need to stop and take notice. Learning to be more mindful and aware can do wonders for our well-being in all areas of life – like our walk to work, the way we eat or our relationships. It helps us get in tune with our feelings and stops us dwelling on the past or worrying about the future – so we get more out of the day-to-day.

Q: When do you stop and take notice?

TRYING OUT: keep learning new things

Learning affects our well-being in lots of positive ways. It exposes us to new ideas and helps us stay curious and engaged. It also gives us a sense of accomplishment and helps boost our self-confidence and resilience. There are many ways to learn new things – not just through formal qualifications. We can share a skill with friends, join a club, learn to sing, play a new sport and so much more.

Q: What new things have you tried recently?

DIRECTION: have goals to look forward to

Feeling good about the future is important for our happiness. We all need goals to motivate us and these need to be challenging enough to excite us, but also achievable. If we try to attempt the impossible this brings unnecessary stress. Choosing ambitious but realistic goals gives our lives direction and brings a sense of accomplishment and satisfaction when we achieve them.

Q: What are your most important goals?

RESILIENCE: find ways to bounce back

All of us have times of stress, loss, failure or trauma in our lives. But how we respond to these has a big impact on our well-being. We often cannot choose what happens to us, but in principle we can choose our own attitude to what happens. In practice it's not always easy, but one of the most exciting findings from recent research is that resilience, like many other life skills, can be learned.

Q: How do you bounce back in tough times?

EMOTION: take a positive approach

Positive emotions – like joy, gratitude, contentment, inspiration and pride – are not just great at the time. Recent research shows that regularly experiencing them creates an 'upward spiral', helping to build our resources. So although we need to be realistic about life's ups and downs, it helps to focus on the good aspects of any situation – the glass half full rather than the glass half empty.

Q: What are you feeling good about?

ACCEPTANCE: be comfortable with who you are

No-one's perfect. But so often we compare our insides to other people's outsides. Dwelling on our flaws – what we're not rather than what we've got – makes it much harder to be happy. Learning to accept ourselves, warts and all, and being kinder to ourselves when things go wrong, increases our enjoyment of life, our resilience and our well-being. It also helps us accept others as they are.

Q: What is the real you like?

MEANING: be part of something bigger

People who have meaning and purpose in their lives are happier, feel more in control and get more out of what they do. They also experience less stress, anxiety and depression. But where do we find 'meaning and purpose'? It might be our religious faith, being a parent or doing a job that makes a difference. The answers vary for each of us but they all involve being connected to something bigger than ourselves.

Q: What gives your life meaning?

⇨ The above information is reprinted with kind permission from Action for Happiness. Please visit www.actionforhappiness.org for further information.

© Action for Happiness 2014

Key facts

⇨ Half of the people who have depression will only experience it once but for the other half it will happen again. The length of time that it takes to recover ranges from around six months to a year or more. (page 1)

⇨ 47% of people personally know someone who has suffered from depression. 21% of people personally know someone who has suffered from anxiety. (page 3)

⇨ The most common mental illnesses are anxiety and depression (22% of the population). (page 6)

⇨ When asked if depression was a medical condition, from the people polled 81% think that depression is a medical condition, 11% think that depression is not a medical condition and 8% were not sure. (page 6)

⇨ One in ten new mothers are affected by postnatal depression. One in 14 new fathers are affected by postnatal depression (Family Lives, 2014). (page 12)

⇨ Shorter days in the winter cause some people to develop a form of depression known as seasonal affective disorder (SAD). (page 13)

⇨ Teenage boys who have a combination of depressive symptoms and raised levels of the stress hormone cortisol are up to 14 times more likely to develop clinical depression than those who show neither trait. (page 14)

⇨ Around one in six people suffer from clinical depression at some point in their lives and three-quarters of mental health diseases start before people are 24 years old. (page 14)

⇨ The research reveals that long-term unemployed young people are more than twice as likely as their peers to have been prescribed antidepressants. (page 15)

⇨ Around half of teens who experience a brief episode of depression or anxiety do not go on to have a mental illness in adulthood, according to a study from the Murdoch Children's Research Institute. (page 16)

⇨ Half of girls and almost one-third of boys have an episode of depression or anxiety in their teens but rates drop sharply when young people reach their 20s. (page 16)

⇨ 34% of 16–25-year-olds in the UK say they have felt depressed as a direct result of something they have viewed on a social networking website. Young women are more likely to be negatively affected by posts they have seen on social networks. (page 18)

⇨ The Royal College of Psychiatrists estimates that 50-65% of people treated with an antidepressant for depression will see an improvement, compared to 25-30% of those taking inactive 'dummy' pills (placebos). (page 19)

⇨ Antidepressants usually need to be taken for 2-4 weeks (without missing a dose) before the benefit is felt. (page 20)

⇨ In England, antidepressant prescriptions increased by ten per cent a year between 1998 and 2010 and in the US, 11% of over-11s were prescribed antidepressant drugs. (page 23)

⇨ Taking a brisk walk may sound old-fashioned, but studies have shown that regular exercise can help you feel better, and sometimes prevent depression developing in the first place. (page 24)

⇨ New research shows that cognitive behavioural therapy, when used along with usual care, can be as effective in patients who don't respond to medication. (page 27)

⇨ Professor Christopher Williams from Glasgow University, said depressed people who were given self-help literature along with sessions advising them how to use the books, had 'lower levels' of depression after a year. (page 31)

⇨ Short spells in a green space does improve people's mood and cognitive functioning. (page 35)

⇨ SPARX, [a computer program that helps young people with mild to moderate depression], was as effective as standard care for adolescents 12– to 19-years-old seeking help for depression. (page 37)

Antidepressants

These include tricyclic antidepressants (TCAs), selective serotonin re-uptake inhibitors (SSRIs) and monoamine oxidase inhibitors (MAOIs). Antidepressants work by boosting one or more chemicals (neurotransmitters) in the nervous system, which may be present in insufficient amounts during a depressive illness.

Anxiety

Feeling nervous, worried or distressed, sometimes to a point where the person feels so overwhelmed that they find everyday life very difficult to handle.

Bipolar disorder

Previously called manic depression, this is an illness where a person can have extreme mood swings where periods of severe depression are balanced by periods of excitement and over activity (mania).

Cognitive behavioural therapy (CBT)

A psychological treatment that assumes that behavioural and emotional reactions are learned over a long period. A cognitive therapist will seek to identify the source of emotional problems and develop techniques to overcome them (helping to change negative though patterns to more positive ones).

Counselling

Sometimes known as talk therapy, allows people to talk through their emotions and their decisions to hurt themselves. The counsellor or therapist provides support and may be able to teach self-harmer how to make more healthy choices in the future.

Depression

Someone is said to be significantly depressed, or suffering from depression, when feelings of sadness or misery don't go away quickly and are so bad that they interfere with everyday life. Symptoms can also include low self-esteem and a lack of motivation. Depression can be triggered by a traumatic/difficult event (reactive depression), but not always (e.g. endogenous depression).

Group therapy

These are meetings for people who are seeking help for a problem (in this case, self-harm or suicidal thoughts) and are led by trained specialists who provide professional advice and support.

Light therapy

A treatment for seasonal affective disorder (SAD) which involves sitting near a light box for up to an hour a day.

Medication

If a person is diagnosed with a mental illness such as clinical depression, medication may be prescribed (see Antidepressants). Some people might not want to take medication at all and prefer talking therapies, whilst others find a combination of both works best for them.

Mental health

Sometimes called 'psychological well-being' or 'emotional health', mental health refers to the state of your mind and how a person can cope with everyday life. It is just as important as good physical health.

Postnatal depression

Depression experienced by new mothers (but new fathers can experience it too). It is not known for certain what causes it, but some experts believe the sudden change in hormones after a baby's birth may be the trigger. Symptoms may include panic attacks, sleeping difficulties, overwhelming fear of death and feelings of inadequacy/being unable to cope.

Seasonal affective disorder (SAD)

A type of depression which generally coincides with the approach of winter and is linked to shortening of daylight hours and lack of sunlight.

Self-help/self-help groups

A group of people, who all self-harm, meet regularly to give each other emotional support and practical advice. Just sharing your problems in a group can help you to feel less alone – others in the group will almost certainly have had similar experiences.

St John's Wort (Hypericum)

A yellow-flowered plant that has been used for centuries as a mild antidepressant.

Talking therapies

These involve talking and listening. Some therapists will aim to find the root cause of a sufferer's problem and help them deal with it, some will help to change behaviour and negative thoughts, while others simply offer support.

Assignments

Brainstorming

⇨ In small groups, discuss what you know about depression. Consider the following points:

- What is the difference between low mood and depression?

- Depression affects people in different ways and can cause a wide variety of symptoms. What are the symptoms associated with depression?

- What is Generalised Anxiety Disorder (GAD) and how does it relate to depression?

Research

⇨ Research the support available for people experiencing depression in your local area. Make a list of any support groups, charities or organisations that you discover and feedback to your class. Consider whether you think there is enough support available, and whether it is easily accessible.

⇨ According to a YouGov survey commissioned by The Prince's Trust, over a third (34%) of young people have felt depressed because of something they have seen on a social network site (see *Negative effects of social networking* on page 18). Create your own survey and find out if anyone in your year group has experienced negative effects of social networking, such as cyberbullying, and how it made them feel. Create graphs from the data and present your findings to the class.

⇨ Watch the video *I had a black dog, his name was depression*, written, illustrated and narrated by Matthew Johnstone (https://www.youtube.com/watch?v=XiCrniLQGYc). 'The black dog' is used as a metaphor for depression, a term Winston Churchill used to refer to his own depression. Research some other terms people have used to describe the illness. What do you think is the most apt description of depression?

⇨ Many artists and writers have suffered from depression, from Vincent Van Gogh to Sylvia Plath. Do you think there a link between depression and creativity? Explore and discuss in groups.

⇨ Music therapy is sometimes used to help depression sufferers. From your music collection, create a 'feel-good playlist' of all the songs which help you when you are feeling low. Why do you think you find listening to these songs therapeutic?

Design

⇨ Seasonal Affective Disorder (SAD) affects around two million people in the UK. Design a poster that explains what SAD is and suggest ways people can combat the 'winter blues'.

⇨ Design a leaflet for teens that details the difference between minor, moderate and clinical depression and the suitable treatment available for each level of depression (e.g. when is self-help or medication appropriate?).

⇨ Design a poster that illustrates the different types of depression identified in the article on pages 1, 2 and 3.

⇨ Recently a number of games have been developed to raise awareness of mental health conditions and how to treat them, such as Depression Quest and SPARX. Read *What is SPARX?* (pages 36 and 37) and use this as a starting point to create you own game or app to help with depression.

Oral

⇨ As a class, stage a debate and consider the question 'Is depression a disability'?

⇨ Read the article *Stigma and discrimination* (pages 6 and 7). Stigma is experienced by people who are affected by depression when negative judgements are made about them based on their condition, usually as a result of stereotypes, misconceptions or fear. Discuss the stereotypes surrounding depression and think about how people diagnosed with depression might be treated because of this.

⇨ 'What is sometimes diagnosed as depression is often just sadness, a normal emotion which we should all expect to feel at times.' Discuss.

⇨ Choose one of the illustrations from this book and, with a partner, discuss what you think the artist was trying to portray.

Reading/writing

⇨ Watch the film *Silver Linings Playbook* (2012) (rated 15), starring Bradley Cooper and Jennifer Lawrence, then write a report discussing how the film represents the issue of depression.

⇨ Read *The Perks of Being a Wallflower* by Stephen Chobosky and/or watch the film of the same name (2012) (rated 12a). How is the issue of depression presented? If you view both mediums, compare and contrast how each different medium explores the issue of depression.

⇨ Read the article *Pros and cons of medication* (pages 21 and 22). Write a short essay which discusses the pros and cons of taking medication to help combat depression. You might want to look at alternatives to drug treatment, such as alternative medicine (e.g. St. John's Wort), talking therapies, exercise, etc.

⇨ Exercise programmes are sometimes recommended as a treatment for mild to moderate depression. Investigate the links between exercise and mental health then write an exercise plan for a person who has depression.

acceptance and happiness 39
acupuncture 29
alcohol 3
Anderson, William 30
antidepressants 4, 19–22
    and postnatal depression 13
    and SAD 11
anxiety 3, 17

biomarker for depression in teenage boys 14
bipolar disorder 1–2, 9–10
boys
    biomarker for depression 14
    difficulty talking about problems 28

causes of depression 1
CBT see cognitive behavioural therapy
cities, benefits of green spaces 35
Close, Glenn 9–10
cognitive behavioural therapy (CBT) 4, 24, 26, 27, 34
    computer program 36–7
    and SAD 11
combination therapy 22
complementary medicine 3, 11, 25
computer program for CBT 36–7
cortisol 14
counselling 4, 24, 26, 29
    postnatal depression 13
couple-focused therapy 26
cyberbullying 18

daylight lamps and SAD 11
depression 1–18
    causes 1
    as a disability 5
    as physical illness 8
    signs and symptoms 1
    types 1–2
diet 3, 24–5
    and SAD 11
direction and happiness 39
Disability Discrimination Act 5
disclosure of depression 5
discrimination 5, 6–7

emotions and happiness 39
exercise see physical activity
experiences of depression 8, 9–10, 34

feelings
    of depression 8
    positive emotions and happiness 39
financial worries 2

general anxiety disorder (GAD) 17
getting help 3–4
giving and happiness 38
goals and happiness 38

GPs 3–4
GREAT DREAM keys to happier living 38–9
green spaces, mental health benefits 35

happiness keys 38–9
homeopathic remedies and SAD 11

institutionalised discrimination 6–7
insurance companies and discrimination 7
Internet friendships 18
interpersonal therapy 24, 26

jobless young people and mental illness 15

late night light exposure and depression 13
learning and happiness 39

major depression 1
MAOIs (monoamine oxidase inhibitors) 20
media stigmatising of mental illness 7
medical help 3–4
medication see antidepressants
men, difficulty talking about problems 28
mental health teams 22
mild depression 1
    treatment options 22
mindfulness based cognitive therapy 26
money worries 2
monoamine oxidase inhibitors (MAOIs) 20

NHS treatment statistics 25
night-time exposure to light 13
non-disclosure of mental illness 7

online bullying 18
over-diagnosis of depression 23

personal relationships
    and happiness 38
    importance of 2
    problems 3
physical activity
    benefits 3, 22, 24, 33, 34, 38
    no evidence of benefit 32
positive attitude 2, 39
postnatal depression 2, 12–13
problem-solving therapy 26
psychodynamic therapy 24, 26
psychotherapy 4
purpose in life and happiness 39

Rainbow SPARX 37
relationships see personal relationships
resilience and happiness 39

SAD (seasonal affective disorder) 2, 11
same/both-sex attracted youth, computerised CBT 37
seasonal affective disorder (SAD) 2, 11
selective serotonin reuptake inhibitors (SSRIs) 20
self-exclusion 7
self-help 2
self-help books 31
self-help groups 22
serotonin-adrenaline reuptake inhibitors (SNRIs) 20
side effects of antidepressants 20, 21
signs and symptoms
  of anxiety 17
  of depression 1
  of postnatal depression 12
SNRIs (serotonin-adrenaline reuptake inhibitors) 20
social networking, negative effects 18
social networks see personal relationships
SPARX 36–7
SSRIs (selective serotonin reuptake inhibitors) 20
St John's Wort 3, 25
statistics
  attitudes to mental illness 6
  NHS referrals and treatment 25
stigma of depression 6–7
stoke 30–31
suicidal thinking and antidepressants 21–2
surfing 30–31
symptoms see signs and symptoms

talking therapies 4, 22, 24, 26
TCAs (tricyclic antidepressants) 20
teenage boys, biomarker for depression 14
treatments 19–37
  postnatal depression 12–13
  SAD 11
  young people 17, 36–7
tricyclic antidepressants (TCAs) 20

unemployment and symptoms of mental illness 15
urban green spaces, mental health benefits 35

Wave Project 30–31
well-being
  keys to happier living 38–9
  and urban green spaces 35
work pressures 2
Wu, Venzen 31

young people and depression 16–17
  and antidepressants 21–2
  and social networking 18
  treatment using SPARX computer program 36–7
  and unemployment 15

Acknowledgements

The publisher is grateful for permission to reproduce the material in this book. While every care has been taken to trace and acknowledge copyright, the publisher tenders its apology for any accidental infringement or where copyright has proved untraceable. The publisher would be pleased to come to a suitable arrangement in any such case with the rightful owner.

Images

Cover, page iii and page 28: iStock, page 4: iStock, page 16 © iStock, page 19 © Jackie Staines, page 26: iStock, page 27: iStock, page 32: iStock, page 37 © Jirka Matousek, pages 38 and 39: iStock.

Illustrations

Don Hatcher: pages 9 & 29. Simon Kneebone: pages 7 & 23. Angelo Madrid: pages 2 & 24.

Additional acknowledgements

Editorial on behalf of Independence Educational Publishers by Cara Acred.

With thanks to the Independence team: Mary Chapman, Sandra Dennis, Christina Hughes, Jackie Staines and Jan Sunderland.

Cara Acred

Cambridge

May 2014